D1575327

THE LIFE OF MARK TWAIN

THE EARLY YEARS

The Life of
MARK TWAIN

THE EARLY YEARS
1835–1871

Gary Scharnhorst

UNIVERSITY OF MISSOURI PRESS
Columbia

Library of Congress Cataloging-in-Publication Data

Names: Scharnhorst, Gary, author.
Title: The life of Mark Twain : the early years, 1835-1871 / by Gary
    Scharnhorst.
Description: Columbia : University of Missouri Press, [2018] | Series: Mark
    Twain and his circle | Includes bibliographical references and index. |
    Identifiers: LCCN 2017044383 (print) | LCCN 2017050629 (ebook) | ISBN
    9780826274007 (e-book) | ISBN 9780826221445 (hardcover : alk. paper)
Subjects: LCSH: Twain, Mark, 1835-1910. | Twain, Mark, 1835-1910--Homes and
    haunts. | Authors, American--19th century--Biography. | Humorists,
    American--19th century--Biography.
Classification: LCC PS1331 (ebook) | LCC PS1331 .S24 2018 (print) | DDC
    818/.409 [B] --dc23
LC record available at https://lccn.loc.gov/2017044383

Typefaces: Clarendon and Jenson

This book was published with the generous support of

The Missouri Humanities Council

and

The State Historical Society of Missouri

Mark Twain and His Circle
Tom Quirk and John Bird, Series Editors

In memory of my father

Contents

Illustrations

Preface

Over a century and a half ago, a columnist for the San Francisco *Dramatic Chronicle* predicted that Samuel Langhorne Clemens, aka Mark Twain, was "bound to have a biographer one of these days—may it be a hundred years hence!" Albert Bigelow Paine's official biography of the author was published less than fifty years later. It is an indispensable source for the legend of Saint Mark. Paine portrayed his subject as "the zealous champion of justice and liberty" who was "never less than fearless and sincere. Invariably he was for the oppressed. He had a natural instinct for the right, but, right or wrong, he was for the underdog." As recently as 2002, Robert E. Weir echoed the dubious claim: Sam Clemens "was an indefatigable foe of anything that stood in the way of human progress and individual potential," as if to suggest that the world would be a better place if only everyone emulated him. Sam's most honest comments about his life, or so he asserted, are in his autobiography, most of which appeared posthumously. "A book that is not to be published for a century gives the writer a freedom which he could secure in no other way," he explained in an interview in 1899. "In these conditions you can draw a man without prejudice exactly as you knew him and yet have no fear of hurting his feelings or those of his sons or grandsons." Similarly, in the autobiography he noted, "I speak from the grave rather than with my living tongue, for a good reason: I can speak thence freely." And in a March 1904 letter to his friend W. D. Howells, Sam described his autobiography as

the truest of all books; for while it inevitably consists mainly in extinctions of the truth, shirkings of the truth, partial revealments of the truth, with hardly an instance of plain straight truth, the remorseless truth is there, between the lines, where the author-cat is raking dust upon it which hides from the disinterested spectator neither it nor its smell . . . the result being that the reader knows the author in spite of his wily diligences.

Howells replied skeptically: "Even you won't tell the black heart's-truth. The man who could do it would be famed to the last day."[1]

Howells was correct. In the end, Sam failed to tell the whole truth and nothing but the truth about his life in his memoirs. From the beginning he was reticent to discuss sex, for example. "There were the Rousseau confessions," he acknowledged, "but I am going to leave that kind alone." He eventually conceded to Howells that "as to veracity" the entire autobiography "was a failure; [Sam] had begun to lie, and that if no man ever yet told the truth about himself it was because no man ever could." Sam elsewhere declared that "no man dares tell the truth until after he is dead." His autobiography is so rife with inaccuracies, embellishments, exaggerations, and utter untruths that a cottage industry of naysayers has developed to debunk it. Many parts contain not so much a remembrance of things past but a remembrance of things that did not happen. As Louis J. Budd remarks, scholars who try "to separate truth from yarn-spinning in his autobiographical dictation" have discovered it is "a mountain of funny putty." Sam Clemens's biographers must consult the autobiography with caution in reconstructing the events of his life. He never allowed the facts to interfere with a good story, such as the discovery of a blind lead in *Roughing It* (1872) or his complicity in the death of a stranger in "The Private History of a Campaign That Failed" (1885). Even the apologetic Paine admitted that Sam's autobiographical dictations bear "only an atmospheric relation to history." Bernard DeVoto agreed that though Sam was one "of the most autobiographical of writers," he was "least autobiographical" when he tried to chronicle his life. Howard Baetzhold describes Sam's memory as "faulty" and "convenient," Hamlin Hill calls it "immensely selective," and James M. Cox refers tactfully to "the magnifying lens of his imagination."[2]

The first task of Sam Clemens's biographers, in short, should be to sort facts from factoids or truth from truthiness, a process akin to stripping lacquer from a painting to reveal the original pigments or removing carpet to expose the grain in a hardwood floor. As Sam famously joked, when he was young "I could remember anything, whether it happened or not," but as he grew older his memories began to fade "and soon I shall be so I cannot remember any but the latter."[3] To arrive at some reliable account of various events, such as Sam's first lecture engagement in San Francisco in early October 1866 or his putative visit to the czar's dacha in Yalta in 1867, I have had to cross-check many sources. He seems to have been a yarn spinner from an early age. As his mother once allowed, "He is the wellspring of truth, but you can't bring up the whole well with one bucket. . . . I discount him 30 per cent for embroidery, and what is left is perfect and priceless truth."[4]

In a Virginia City, Nevada, *Territorial Enterprise* column in January 1863, the month before adopting the Mark Twain pseudonym, Sam conceded that, on his part, he had "a sort of talent for posturing." As Ron Powers remarks, "he was forever revising his life to make it even more interesting and melodramatic than it had been." Many Clemens scholars note the extent to which he crafted his own reputation or, as Jeffrey Steinbrink has observed, "anybody who attempts a biography" of Sam collaborates with him, since he "was in the process of constructing himself . . . throughout his career." Hill similarly observes that "if art is a mode of dissembling, the Samuel Clemens hidden beneath his own disguise was an artist of a magnitude as yet not completely defined and barely explored." Not even Sam's travel books—*The Innocents Abroad* (1869), *Roughing It* (1872), *A Tramp Abroad* (1880), *Life on the Mississippi* (1883), and *Following the Equator* (1897)—are entirely reliable sources about his life, despite his insistence that if "the incidents were dated, they could be strung together in their due order, & the result would be an autobiography." On the contrary: Hill refers, for example, to Twain's "enormous violation of the facts of his biography" in the construction of his narrative persona in *Roughing It*. Put another way, virtually all of his major works, including his autobiography, are semiautobiographical. If, on the one hand, I've depended as little as possible on these narratives and have explicitly acknowledged my debt when it has been necessary to cite them, on the other hand the statement underscores the pressing need for a complete and reliable biography of the author for what it tells us about the alchemy of his imagination. "I never deliberately sat down and 'created' a character in my life," Sam told an interviewer in 1907. "I begin to write incidents out of real life."[5]

Sam Clemens enjoys a reputation unrivaled in American literary history, and he was in large part the architect of that reputation. From the start of his career, he tried to control his public image. As early as 1871 a columnist in the *Phrenological Journal* commended Sam's marketing genius, noting that he "is shrewd, and not only understands how to write and name a book, but also how to advertise it." Sam understood intuitively the advantages of favorable publicity, and he was adept at "dramatizing his celebrity," Budd comments. In "both a literary and psychological sense, the shambling but perceptive humorist remembered as Mark Twain is a mask," according to Louis Leary, a "posturing and flamboyant figure" created by Clemens, who over the years sculpted his public persona and fiercely protected it. Budd has explained that Sam "did not just welcome publicity: he eagerly sought it for almost fifty years." He readily sat for interviews when they were to his advantage, as when they served to promote a book or lecture, but otherwise he was largely inaccessible. He praised his butler for learning to lie when turning away "the newspaper correspondent or the visitor at the front door." He often admonished interviewers not to publish his exact words because he could sell them for up to thirty cents apiece rather than give them away. "Don't print a word of what I have said," he ordered a stringer for the New York *World* in November 1900. "It is my trade to gaggle, and if I talk to reporters for nothing where's my bread and butter coming in?" In 1903 he claimed, "To

ask a man who writes for his livelihood to talk for publication without rec-
ompense is an injustice." He never employed a publicist because he didn't
need one—or, more correctly, he saw one in the mirror. He sometimes urged
his correspondents to destroy his private letters rather than jeopardize his
public image, as in a postscript he sent his brother Orion and Orion's wife
Mollie as early as October 1865, a month before his thirtieth birthday, even
before his comic sketch "Jim Smiley and His Jumping Frog" appeared in
the New York *Saturday Press*: "You had best shove this in the stove" because
"I don't want any absurd 'literary remains' & 'unpublished letters of Mark
Twain' published after I am planted." Similarly, he admonished his mother
and sister in January 1868, over two years later and some sixteen months
before the publication of *The Innocents Abroad*, his first great literary and
commercial success, to read his letter "*only* to the family, & then burn it—I
do *hate* to have anybody know anything about my business." Ironically, these
letters not only survive, but the texts have been published—not that Sam
would have been surprised. Shortly after the birth of his youngest daughter
in 1880, he interrupted a note to his friend Joseph Twichell to admonish the
future reader of his private correspondence, noting that

> somebody may be reading *this* letter 80 years hence. And so, my friend (you
> pitying snob, I mean, who are holding this yellow paper in your hand in 1960,)
> save yourself the trouble of looking further; I know how pathetically trivial
> our small concerns would seem to you, & I will not let your eye profane them.
> No, I keep my news; you keep your compassion. Suffice it you to know, scoffer
> & ribald, that the little child is old & blind, now, & once more toothless; &
> the rest of us are shadows, these many, many years.[6]

This pattern of massaging the message and spin-doctoring holds throughout
Sam's life. Late in his career he hired a clipping service, and the files of the
Mark Twain Papers at the University of California–Berkeley are filled with
the articles he was sent. Most of his interviews in Australasia and South Af-
rica in 1895–96 are known to scholarship only because newspaper clippings
of them survive in his scrapbooks.

In the course of his long career Sam Clemens lost as many friends as he
made. He did not suffer fools or rivals gladly, especially if they wore crino-
line. He targeted them indiscriminately—from religious leaders (e.g., John
Alexander Dowie, Mary Baker Eddy, De Witt Talmage), politicians (William McKinley, Theodore Roosevelt, Tim Sullivan), and fellow writers and
lecturers (Bret Harte, Kate Field) to literary pirates (John Camden Hotten)
and military leaders (Frederick Funston). If Sam was often loved in public,
he was sometimes loathed in private. He feuded for years with C. C. Dun-
can, the captain of the *Quaker City*, the ship that carried him and the other

"innocents" to Europe and the Holy Land in 1867. Though he and James were both friends with Howells, neither of them could abide the other's work. If Henry James was "the Master," a careful craftsman who considered Sam's writings vulgar, then Sam was the anti-James, an improvisational artist who, he said, "would rather be damned to John Bunyan's heaven" than read *The Bostonians*.[7]

Particularly early in his career, Sam systematically burlesqued all types of fiction and journalism (e.g., temperance literature, French and epistolary novels, gothic and ghost stories, dime and detective novels, fairy tales, success stories, joke books, almanacs, theatrical reviews, sentimental romances, travel narratives, biography and autobiography, pornography, fashion articles, obituaries, interviews, medicinal and lovelorn advice columns, news reports, social columns, sportswriting, and celebrity features) as well as popular plays, operatic librettos, and Shakespearean comedies and tragedies. His hoaxes and parodies gradually evolved into social and political satire. But everything he wrote did not turn to gold, nor was every speech he delivered touched with genius. He readily violated the classical unities and ignored the standards of the well-made novel. Or, as Howells remarked,

> he was not enslaved to the consecutiveness in writing which the rest of us try to keep chained to. That is, he wrote as he thought, and as all men think, without sequence, without an eye to what went before or should come after. If something beyond or beside what he was saying occurred to him, he invited it into his page, and made it as much at home there as the nature of it would suffer him.[8]

While *Adventures of Huckleberry Finn* (1885) is generally hailed as a great American novel, Sam also suffered his share of reverses and disasters. He was hardly exempt from the slings and arrows of outraged critics. He published his share of flops and potboilers, such as *Merry Tales* (1892), *The American Claimant* (1892), and *Tom Sawyer Abroad* (1894), all written when he was in the throes of financial exigency and imminent bankruptcy. All of these books clearly fall below the mark of his best writing. A consummate performer in his own right, he nevertheless wrote with Bret Harte the play *Ah Sin* (1877), the most disastrous collaboration in the history of American letters. Ambitious to succeed, he was notoriously unwise in his investments, thinking the telephone a wildcat speculation while backing such inventions as a steam pulley, a carpet pattern machine, and a powdered food supplement made from the albumin of eggs called plasmon. In short, he exhibited his share of human foibles, despite his modern reputation.

Over the decades, the field of Samuel Clemens biography has often resembled a bloody battleground. The most famous critical war occurred in the late 1920s and 1930s between the first two curators of the Mark Twain Papers, Paine and DeVoto, with Clemens's surviving daughter and heir, Clara, a self-interested spectator. In 1906 Clemens commissioned Paine, a young sycophant without a pedigree, to write his official biography. After Clemens's death in 1910 Paine managed the papers with the goal of maximizing their profitability to the Mark Twain Company and his estate by churning out a steady stream of Twain-related books and magazine articles based on materials in the archive: the hagiographical *Mark Twain: A Biography* (1912) and bowdlerized editions of *Mark Twain's Letters* (1917), *Mark Twain's Speeches* (1923), *Mark Twain's Autobiography* (1924), and *Mark Twain's Notebook* (1935). Thomas Sergeant Perry once disparaged the archival method of compiling such magisterial works. "The biographer," he wrote, "gets a dustcart into which he shovels diaries, reminiscences, old letters, until the cart is full. Then he dumps the load in front of your door. That is Vol. I. Then he goes forth again on the same errand. And there is Vol. II. Out of this rubbish the reader constructs a biography." Paine tightly controlled access to the manuscripts; that is, his proprietary interest in Mark Twain was at least as pronounced as Leon Edel's in Henry James a couple of generations later. Paine was a gatekeeper, and among those he denied entry was DeVoto, a young Harvard University graduate who believed that Van Wyck Brooks had distorted the record by contending in the thesis-ridden *The Ordeal of Mark Twain* (1920) that Sam's native genius had been repressed and his writings censored by his genteel wife Olivia "Livy" Langdon Clemens, editors, and friends. As Brooks suggested most succinctly, "the making of the humorist was the undoing of the artist." Without rehearsing this controversy or his conflict with Paine in detail, DeVoto needed to examine the original manuscripts in order to dispute Brooks's thesis, but Paine colluded with Harper & Bros., Sam's last publisher, to refuse DeVoto access to the papers. As he advised the editors at the House of Harper, "on general principles it is a mistake to let anyone else write about Mark Twain, as long as we can prevent it. . . . As soon as this is begun (writing about him at all, I mean) the Mark Twain that we have 'preserved'—the Mark Twain that we knew, the traditional Mark Twain—will begin to fade and change, and with that process the Harper Mark Twain property will depreciate." In his introduction to a 1980 reprinting of the authorized biography, James M. Cox concludes unequivocally that Paine "acted as censor and custodian," doing all he could to preserve the life he had written and unhesitatingly denying would-be revisionists like DeVoto access to the papers. Ironically, Paine appropriated some of Sam's manuscripts for his personal use without permission, and carelessly lost other documents, including the manuscript of Orion Clemens's autobiography. In the foreword to *Mark Twain's*

America (1932), DeVoto expressed scorn for Paine's motives and methods. When he was starting to research his book, according to DeVoto, Paine informed him that "nothing more need ever be written about Mark Twain. The canon was established, and whatever biography or criticism had to say could be found in the six pounds of letterpress that composed Mr. Paine's official Life." DeVoto observed that the furor caused by Brooks's thesis "rested on one marginal note quoted by Mr. Paine which accused [the primary scapegoat, Olivia Langdon Clemens] of steadily weakening the English language." DeVoto eventually concluded, too, that Sam—not Livy, Howells, or his other ostensible censors—"was responsible for many of the euphemisms and avoidances" in his writings. Paine delivered his patronizing reply in the preface to the centenary edition of *Mark Twain: A Biography* (1935): DeVoto seemed "a young man . . . more talented than exact" and "not always pleased with the facts as he finds them. . . . The young man plainly was not pleased with Mark Twain's choice of those to whom he trusted his literary effects— his daughter, Clara, and the writer of these lines."[9] Ironically, in the same year DeVoto also began to contribute a popular column, "The Easy Chair," to *Harper's Monthly*, and in 1938, the year after Paine's death, he was selected to succeed him as curator of the Mark Twain Papers. He remained in this office until 1946, and before his own death in 1955 he had received both a Pulitzer Prize for history and a National Book Award for nonfiction.

Nevertheless, Brooks's contention that Sam had been crippled artistically by the censors who surrounded him, including his wife Livy, editor Howells, and his friend Mary Mason Fairbanks, had the effect of fostering the false notion that Mark Twain was his alter ego or that he suffered from a multiple personality disorder like Dr. Jekyll and Mr. Hyde. Twain biography became and has remained a fertile field for psychoanalytically inclined critics. In Freudian terms, if "the Wild Humorist of the Pacific Slope" (Twain) was the id, then the bourgeois family man who resided in a Victorian mansion (Clemens) was the superego. "The solution for critics . . . at least since Brooks," according to Richard S. Lowry, has been to resolve the contradictions in his character "by literally dividing him in two." Arthur G. Pettit alludes darkly to his "multiple personality." Even DeVoto, Brooks's most vocal opponent, conceded that "for a time" after the death of his wife and favorite daughter, Sam "lived perilously close to the indefinable line between sanity and madness." Paul Fatout epitomized this tendency toward armchair psychoanalysis when he tried to gauge precisely the "vague and shifting" line "where Clemens yields to Twain and vice versa," as if there were "two persons occupying the same body," which is exactly what Andrew Hoffman asserted in his biography *Inventing Mark Twain* (1997). Forrest G. Robinson flirts with the same notion by claiming that "the line separating Clemens from

Twain was far from clear," even "to the man who bore those names," though Robinson immediately qualifies his point by affirming a more conventional view: "Clemens was a historical person of many and complex dimensions, but there was only one of him. Mark Twain was a fiction of many and complex dimensions—not the least of them his relationship to his maker—but he was a fiction."[10] That is, his ego was more intact than many critics have been willing to grant.

In short, for decades after the publication of *The Ordeal of Mark Twain*, Brooks's thesis skewed the field of Clemens studies. In his 1930 Nobel Prize acceptance speech in Stockholm, Sinclair Lewis betrayed Brooks's influence when he declared that Howells "was actually able to tame Mark Twain, perhaps the greatest of our writers, and to put that fiery old savage into an intellectual frock coat and top hat." According to Justin Kaplan, he was "a double creature": "The Hartford literary gentleman lived inside the sagebrush bohemian." The very title of Kaplan's *Mr. Clemens and Mark Twain* (1966), a play on Dr. Jekyll and Mr. Hyde, nods in Brooks's direction, as does the milder common critical judgment that Sam was a welter of "contradictions" or "inconsistencies" sometimes verging on the pathological. To cite only a few examples: Gladys Bellamy ("Mark Twain seethed with contradictions"); Edward Wagenknecht ("There are contradictions in Mark Twain's attitude about himself, as in everything else about him"); J. Stanley Mattson ("the contradictions in Mark Twain's character were legion"); Fred Kaplan ("a man of many inconsistencies"); Joseph F. Goeke ("chronic vacillation, impulsiveness, and self-contradiction"); Peter Krass ("a complex man who was almost schizophrenic"); and Margaret Duckett ("Mark Twain contradicted himself on almost every subject"). Gregg Camfield avers that Sam's "attitudes toward the world of commerce seem confused and contradictory," particularly "the contradiction between his support of labor and his investment in a labor-supplanting machine." He was an unabashedly countercultural figure—except when he was not. He also affirmed the standards of the social status quo—except when he did not. While Sam sometimes spoke truth to power, as when he condemned the depredations of the American military in Cuba and the Philippines during the Spanish-American War, he almost as often spoke what he considered truth to powerlessness, as when he sued a poor hack driver for overcharging his maid on a fare and justified his action on the ground of "civic duty."[11] He scorned hypocrisy, but he was vulnerable to accusations of hypocrisy in his own right. By the end of his life he had become both king and court jester, both Lear and the Fool.

In his final years Sam even expressed profound uncertainty about his rank as a writer. On the one hand, he believed that the reputations of such literary comedians as Artemus Ward, Josh Billings, and Petroleum V. Nasby had "perished" after their deaths because "they were merely humorists. Humorists of the 'mere' sort cannot survive. Humor is only a fragrance, a decoration. . . . Humor must not professedly teach, and it must not professedly preach, but it must do both if it would live forever." On his part, he insisted that he had "always preached. That is the reason that I have lasted thirty years." During his final visit to Missouri in 1902 he reiterated the point to an interviewer: "I am a preacher. We are all preachers. If we do not preach by words, we preach by deeds." Put another way, while he was first and foremost a humorist, Sam Clemens was not a humorist exclusively. He even admitted in old age to a worry that he had "only amused people" and that "their laughter has submerged me."[12]

To be sure, Sam was never a systematic thinker, especially on matters of business and finance. He played with ideas the way a jazz musician plays the trumpet. For example, as Forrest Robinson puts it, his "contempt for money was matched by his craving for it." On the one hand, he satirized Cornelius Vanderbilt's predatory capitalism in "Open Letter to Commodore Vanderbilt" (1869), was a founding member in 1891 of the American Friends of Russian Freedom, and supported socialists such as Maxim Gorky. "I'm a revolutionist . . . by birth, breeding principle, and everything else," he told an interviewer in 1906. "I love all revolutions no matter where or when they start." On the other hand, he admired his father-in-law Jervis Langdon, a self-made tycoon, and late in life he hobnobbed with such nabobs as Andrew Carnegie and Henry Huttleston Rogers (aka Hell Hound Rogers to his enemies), vice president of the Standard Oil Company. Howells considered Sam both a "theoretical socialist" and a "practical aristocrat." Justin Kaplan adds that "as a writer he stood outside American society of the Gilded Age, but as a businessman he embraced its business values."[13]

Sam was also an ambivalent or liminal figure in dozens of other ways. He was a popular lecturer who hated lecturing, especially in country villages. Depending on his mood, he could be either a flamboyant showman in a white linen suit or a recluse in pajamas, either a philanthropist or a misanthrope. He was a practical joker, but quick to anger whenever he became the butt of a practical joke. Blessed with an eye for the ironic or absurd, a harsh critic of cant, he was also notoriously prickly. He was both a devoted husband and a negligent father, both a debunker and an inventor of tall tales. He earned vast wealth by writing and lecturing, and lost most of it in wildcat schemes and poor investments. According to John Gerber, he was by turns "an optimist and a pessimist, an idealist and a materialist, a reformer and a determinist." But, to be fair, Sam was no more enigmatic or contradictory a figure than the poet Walt Whitman, who famously proclaimed in section 51 of "Song of Myself," "Do I contradict myself? / Very well, then, I contradict myself. / I am large. I contain multitudes." If, as F. Scott Fitzgerald once said, "the test of a first-rate intelligence is the ability to hold two opposed ideas in mind at the same time and still retain the ability to function," then Sam was an unqualified genius. While he routinely resisted authority, repeatedly challenged the status quo, and earned a reputation for iconoclasm and irreverence, he also enjoyed French cuisine and luxury travel. He was a cultural icon who subverted cultural norms, less a conformist than a counter-counterculturist, so transgressive he sometimes rebelled even against nonconformity. Or, as DeVoto bluntly asserted, "He was anarchy."[14] He harbored divided loyalties, but not a divided psyche. That is, a second task of a Clemens biographer is to avoid the simpleminded view of him as a split personality.

Still, all of his biographers must decide how to refer to him. Some resolve the issue by calling him Sam or Clemens in his youth and Mark or Twain after he adopted the pseudonym in Nevada in 1863. Others use the names interchangeably. It was a problem for Clemens, too. He began to sign some of his letters to his family "Mark" as early as July 1863, yet during his courtship and thirty-five-year marriage to his wife Olivia he always signed his letters to her as Sam. He complained in 1869 that he was often confused with his persona: "I am in some sense a *public* man . . . but my private character is hacked, & dissected, & mixed up with my public one." In 1871 he alluded to his "hated nom de plume (for I do loathe the very sight of it)." For good or ill, the pseudonym became a trademark or brand name and a successful marketing tool. The name was used to sell brands of whiskey, cigars, self-pasting scrapbooks, and shirt collars; he sued publishing pirates not on the grounds of copyright violation but of trademark infringement. After the sales success of *The Innocents Abroad*, his publishers required him to use the pseudonym. The contract he signed with American Publishing Co. of Hartford, Connecticut, in June 1872 for a prospective book on the South African diamond mines (never written) stipulated that he "would receive an 8.5 percent royalty" if it appeared under the name Mark Twain, but "only 5 percent" if he "were to use a different nom de plume." He wanted "A True Story" (1874), his first piece in the *Atlantic Monthly*, and his novel *The Prince and the Pauper* (1881) to appear either without signature or under his real name because neither was a comic tale of the type Mark Twain was known to write and he preferred not to "swindle people" with false advertising of the brand; and, in fact, later in his career he occasionally published "serious" work without signature or under a different pseudonym, including the allegory "The Curious Republic of Gondour" (1875), *Personal Recollections of Joan of Arc* (1896), and *What Is Man?* (1906). He practiced a form of self-erasure, publishing the risqué *1601* (1882) anonymously. "I shall never be accepted seriously over my own signature," he told his biographer Paine. "People always want to laugh over what I write and are disappointed if they don't find a joke in it." In a letter to the editor of the *New York Tribune* in 1871 he endorsed capital punishment but to avoid confusing the public by attaching to it his comic pseudonym, he concealed (if only slightly) his identity by signing it Samuel Langhorne. Near the end of his life he admitted he should have assumed two noms de plume, one for his humor writings, the other for his "serious" work. Even Sam's daughter Susy hated the pseudonym, reportedly telling the novelist Grace King in 1892 that she "should like never to hear it again! My father should not be satisfied with it! He should not be known by it! He should show himself the great writer that he is, not merely a funny man. Funny! That's all the people see in him—a maker of funny speeches!" Howells wrote as late as 1908 that he thought Sam had moved from New York to Connecticut "to get rid of Mark Twain." In short, Mark Twain was always an implied author or public persona or, as Edgar Marquess Branch put it, "Mark Twain was a highly adaptable, partly fictional version of Clemens," an iteration or a pose.[15] That is, Sam Clemens was Twain, but Twain was not Sam Clemens, and so I will refer to him throughout this biography by his given name, not his pen name.

I have saved the most pressing question for last: Why another biography of the author? My best answer is that Paine was unable—for a variety of reasons, not the least of which was his lack of professional training—to write a thoroughly satisfactory biography, even in the space of a half million words, and all Clemens biographers since Paine have tailored their narratives to fit the parameters of a single volume. As Gregg Camfield explains, "The extraordinary amount of information available about his complex life makes any biographer's task almost impossible, so that almost all of them narrow their scope in some significant way." That is, for the past century every Clemens biographer has labored under constraints, like a painter with a small canvas and a limited number of colors on the palette. They have covered Clemens's life selectively or piecemeal, usually by focusing on a period, relationship, or theme. Henry B. Wonham refers to this trend as the "shrinking critical gaze" on Clemens.[16] For example, no fewer than a dozen full-length scholarly biographies have examined his life before his voyage to Europe and the Holy Land aboard the *Quaker City* in 1867: Minnie Brashear's *Mark Twain: Son of Missouri* (1934); Ivan Benson's *Mark Twain's Western Years* (1938); Effie Mona Mack's *Mark Twain in Nevada* (1947); Walter Frear's *Mark Twain in Hawaii* (1947); Dixon Wecter's *Sam Clemens of Hannibal* (1952); Paul Fatout's *Mark Twain in Virginia City* (1964); Edgar Branch's *The Literary Apprenticeship of Mark Twain* (1966); Margaret Sanborn's *Mark Twain: The Bachelor Years* (1990); Nigey Lennon's *The*

Sagebrush Bohemian: Mark Twain in California (1991); Joe Coulombe's *Mark Twain and the American West* (2003); Terrell Dempsey's *Searching for Jim: Slavery in Sam Clemens's World* (2003); and James Caron's *Mark Twain: Unsanctified Newspaper Reporter* (2008). Similarly, John Muller's *Mark Twain in Washington, D.C.* (2013) spotlights Sam's life in the nation's capital during the winter of 1867–68; and a trio of scholarly books have been published devoted to the sliver of Clemens's life in Buffalo, New York, in 1869–71: Jeffrey Steinbrink's *Getting to Be Mark Twain* (1991); Joseph McCullough and Janice McIntire-Strasburg's *Mark Twain at the Buffalo Express* (1999); and Thomas J. Reigstad's *Scribblin' for a Livin': Mark Twain's Pivotal Period in Buffalo* (2013)—though the latter volume inexplicably fails to cite the other two. Kenneth R. Andrews's *Nook Farm: Mark Twain's Hartford Circle* (1969) profiles Sam's years in the Connecticut capital between 1871 and 1891; Robert D. Jerome and Herbert A. Wisbey Jr.'s *Mark Twain in Elmira* (1977) chronicles his twenty summers at his in-laws' homes in the Southern Tier region of New York; Howard G. Baetzhold's *Mark Twain and John Bull: The British Connection* (1970) logs the history of his travels in England; Harry B. Davis's *Mark Twain in Heidelberg* (1985) recounts events during his months in that town on the Neckar River in 1878; and Philip W. Leon's *Mark Twain and West Point* (1996) details his experiences at the military academy and with the cadets. Richard Zacks's *Chasing the Last Laugh: Mark Twain's Raucous and Redemptive Round-the-World Comedy Tour* (2016) chronicles Sam's 1895–96 North American, Australasian, and African lecture trip, and Carl Dolmetsch's *"Our Famous Guest": Mark Twain in Vienna* (1992) his two-year fin de siècle residence in Austria; and Elizabeth Wallace's *Mark Twain and the Happy Island* (1913) and Donald Hoffmann's *Mark Twain in Paradise* (2006) record his experiences in Bermuda, most of them during the last decade of his life. Several volumes focus on Sam's personal associations with and/or intellectual debts to other figures, including Arlin Turner's *Mark Twain and George Washington Cable: The Record of a Literary Friendship* (1960); Margaret Duckett's *Mark Twain and Bret Harte* (1964); Hamlin Hill's *Mark Twain and Elisha Bliss* (1964); Kenneth E. Eble's *Old Clemens and W.D.H.: The Story of a Remarkable Friendship* (1985); Resa Willis's *Mark and Livy: The Love Story of Mark Twain and the Woman Who Almost Tamed Him* (1992); Anthony J. Berret's *Mark Twain and Shakespeare: A Cultural Legacy* (1993); Jason Gary Horn's *Mark Twain and William James: Crafting a Free Self* (1996); Susan K. Harris's *The Courtship of Olivia Langdon and Mark Twain* (1997); Philip Ashley Fanning's *Mark Twain and Orion Clemens: Brothers, Partners, Strangers* (2003); Peter B. Messent's *Mark Twain and Male Friendship: The Twichell, Howells, and Rogers Friendships* (2009); and Forrest G. Robinson, Gabriel Brahm, and Catherine Carlstroem's *The*

Jester and the Sages: Mark Twain in Conversation with Nietzsche, Freud, and Marx (2011). Yet, as Leland Krauth adds, missing from this list "is a biography emphasizing the family life that sees through the sentimental image fostered by Clemens, Livy, and their daughters."[17]

Though most of Sam's life is thoroughly documented, the record is incomplete in several significant ways. The biggest biographical blind spot comprises the hundreds of lost articles he contributed to the Virginia City *Territorial Enterprise* between 1862 and 1866. More specifically, as the San Francisco correspondent of the *Enterprise* between June 1865 and March 1866 Sam sent perhaps 20 letters a month, or a total of about 160 letters, to Washoe, though excerpts from only about one-third of the texts reprinted in other papers have been recovered. In January 1866 Sam reported that he had "burned up a small cart-load" of his sketches clipped from the *Enterprise* and other papers—the metaphor connotes raw ore—because "they were not worth republishing." In March 1870 he mentioned his receipt of a "coffin of 'Enterprise' files" from his brother Orion that have since disappeared. The fire that destroyed the Virginia City business district in October 1875 burned the proprietary copy of the *Territorial Enterprise*. A second file of the *Enterprise*, compiled at a cost of forty thousand dollars and used to document mining titles and afterward donated to the San Francisco Public Library, was destroyed in the fire that followed the San Francisco earthquake in April 1906. As a result, the vast majority of Sam's contributions to the *Enterprise* have been lost. A dozen or so travel letters he mailed from Europe to the San Francisco *Alta California* during the *Quaker City* voyage vanished in the mail, and hundreds of letters he sent his mother over the decades were destroyed in 1904, apparently at his behest.[18] In short, while his life may be reconstructed in extraordinary detail, there are some gaps in the record that may never be filled.

Then there are the biographies that ignore large swaths of Sam's epic life because the whole of it cannot be compressed "into a tidy single volume," as Michael Shelden remarks. Justin Kaplan's *Mr. Clemens and Mark Twain* opens in 1867, with the author at the age of thirty-one on the eve of his departure for Europe aboard the *Quaker City*, on the grounds that Sam was "always his own biographer, and the books he wrote about [his early] years are incomparably the best possible accounts" of them—a demonstrably false assumption. Whereas Kaplan begins his biography with the *Quaker City* voyage, Ron Powers scants the voyage in *Mark Twain: A Life* (2005). Kaplan, Powers, and Jerome Loving in *Mark Twain: The Adventures of Samuel L. Clemens* (2010) also give short shrift to the final years of the life. Still other scholars—Hamlin Hill in *Mark Twain: God's Fool* (1973); William R. Macnaughton in *Mark Twain's Last Years as a Writer* (1979); Karen Lystra in *Dangerous Intimacy: The Untold Story of Mark Twain's Final Years* (2006); Shelden in *Mark Twain: Man in White; The Grand Adventure of the Final Years* (2010); and Laura Skandera-Trombley in *Mark Twain's Other Woman: The Hidden Story of His Final Years* (2010)—focus on his final decade. This patchwork approach has prompted Shelden to argue that "in the absence of a longer, less fragmented narrative that covers all major aspects of the life and works, devoted readers will have to put together their own biographical library made up of the many books focusing on various stages and aspects of the story." Camfield similarly suggests that "perhaps a collection of biographies does the best job of capturing the complexity" of Clemens's life. The argument is reminiscent of Johnny Cash's song "One Piece at a Time," about an autoworker who assembles a grotesque Cadillac entirely from spare parts from different models; that is, it implies that the best Clemens biography might consist of a fuel pump from DeVoto, mud flaps from Powers, airbags from Wecter, a crankshaft from Brooks, a muffler from Paine, and so on. Moreover, some biographers reach wildly different conclusions. Whereas DeVoto insists that Hannibal, Missouri, is "the most important single fact in the life of Samuel Clemens," DeLancey Ferguson claims that from "a literary standpoint" Sam's years on the river "were the four most important years of his life," and Powers asserts that the "steamboat years remained the most hallowed period of his life." Whereas Dahlia Armon and Walter Blair claim that he "clearly was uncomfortable with unconventional female behavior of any sort," Jarrod Roark opines that he just as clearly was attracted "to women who contested sexual mores" and "violated the law." Needless to say, I believe there is a better way: a biography plotted from beginning to end from a single point of view on an expansive canvas. While multivolume biographies of such American authors as Emily Dickinson, Theodore Dreiser, Ralph Waldo Emerson, William Faulkner, Robert Frost, Ernest Hemingway, W. D. Howells, Langston Hughes, Henry James, Herman Melville, and Vladimir Nabokov have appeared in recent years, this life of Samuel Langhorne Clemens is the first multivolume biography of him to appear in over a century—since Paine's hagiography in 1912—and the first multivolume biography of him ever written without apologetic purpose. "If any American writer deserves a modern scholarly biography of two or three large volumes," Shelden has observed, "it is Mark Twain."[19]

Still, there is a related question: What is left to be said? Hasn't the carcass been picked so clean that not a morsel of meat remains on the bones? In fact, no. As Loving has noted, since Kaplan's biography—which received both a Pulitzer Prize and a National Book Award for biography—was published in 1966, "more than five thousand of Mark Twain's letters have been discovered." On average, a hundred Clemens letters and a couple of Clemens interviews new to scholarship surface every year. Moreover, in local U.S. newspapers now available online through the National Digital Newspaper Project funded by the National Endowment for the Humanities, I have located hundreds of new documents relevant to Clemens's life in Missouri, along the Mississippi River, and in the West, including some of the columns Sam contributed to the *Territorial Enterprise* that had been presumed lost. I cannot overstate the importance of the new technology in revolutionizing literary studies. When Albert Bigelow Paine published his official biography of Mark Twain, he believed that no issues of the *Hannibal Journal* for the period when Sam worked for the paper were extant. Today many of those issues are readily available online in digitized format.

Nevertheless, I readily admit that it is not always possible to drill to the bedrock of biographical facts about Sam Clemens. What exactly prompted his acquaintance Robert Collier to hint that the author was guilty of some unspecified impropriety in Bermuda in 1909?[20] It is impossible to know today in the absence of additional documentation. Of course, the lack of corroborating evidence hasn't prevented some biographers from indulging in silly speculation, such as Andrew Hoffman's conjecture in *Inventing Mark Twain* (1997) that Sam and his friend William Wright, aka Dan De Quille, may have had a homosexual relationship when they shared lodgings in Nevada in 1863–64. For Hoffman and others of his ilk, the absence of evidence only betrays the possibility of a cover-up or a conspiracy to conceal the truth. And how can one disprove such a conspiracy without seeming to become a part of it?

A final cautionary note: I endeavor throughout this work to elide the danger of presentism; that is, to resist the temptation to evaluate Sam's life by reinventing him as if he was our contemporary. Shelley Fisher Fishkin makes this mistake when she asserts that Clemens "often strikes us as more a creature of our time than of his." Such a claim begs the truth. It is designed to polish the public reputation of the iconic Mark Twain and render him palatable or politically correct for high school students and visitors to Hannibal and Hartford; these are the very bubbles of pretense he rejoiced in pricking. He embraced some of the petty prejudices that flourished in the milieu of his boyhood for the rest of his life, and he should be viewed in the context of his own time, not ours. While he may have been, as Andrew Levy suggests, "one of the nation's most progressive voices" on race,[21] the statement requires several layers of qualification, including recognition that he harbored an explicable hatred for Indians most of his life, that he never disputed the justice of the *Plessy v. Ferguson* decision of the U.S. Supreme Court in 1896 that sanctioned legal segregation in public facilities, and that he never was a proponent of social or economic equality among the races.

He was not the avuncular figure at the helm of a supertanker portrayed in television commercials or the co(s)mic hero of a *Star Trek* episode or even the humorist represented onstage in a white linen suit and fright wig by Mark Twain impersonators. (How many of these actors realize they are mimicking a middle-aged bankrupt circling the globe on a speaking tour to repay his creditors?) He scarcely deserves his modern reputation as a cracker-barrel philosopher with a ready supply of quips and one-liners, a legacy epitomized by such coffee-table compilations of his maxims as *Mark Twain: Wit and Wisdom* (1935), *The Wit and Wisdom of Mark Twain* (1987), and *The Quotable Mark Twain: His Essential Aphorisms, Witticisms, and Concise Opinions* (1998).

Until the final decade of his life Sam was first and foremost a professional writer who lectured occasionally to support his habit. He reviled the middlemen and -women of literary production who tried to reinvent him or remake him into a polite man of letters. "If I choose to use the language of the vulgar, the low-flung and the sinful, and such as will shock the ears of the highly civilized," he declared in the *Territorial Enterprise* as early as 1864, "I don't want [anyone] to appoint himself an editorial critic and proceed to tone me down." Or, as he wrote to Howells in 1887, "high & fine literature is wine, and mine is only water; but everybody likes water." Or, as he famously insisted to Andrew Lang two years later, "I have been misjudged from the very first. I have never tried in even one single instance to cultivate the cultivated classes. I was not equipped for it, either by native gifts or training. And I never had any ambition in that direction, but always hunted for bigger game—the masses."[22]

The reader of these volumes should expect no bombshells; I expose no dark secrets in Sam Clemens's life. The story is compelling enough without any sensational revelations. I hope that the tale I relate will rise or fall entirely on its merits or lack thereof, not because it reads like a course correction to trends in Mark Twain studies. Few authors have enjoyed a more eventful career than he, and even fewer of their lives can be documented in more detail. Sam was one of the most often quoted, photographed, and interviewed Americans of his era. Howells described him as "the Lincoln of our literature" and referred to "the inexhaustible, the fairy, the Arabian Nights story" of his life. According to Bruce Michelson, his biography "has become a national literary treasure in its own right; for students of American cultural history, that narrative can be the most compelling and significant story associated with his name."[23] He was extraordinarily fortunate to have been born and raised when and where he was; to have become a Mississippi steamship pilot in the heyday of the profession; to have fled the Civil War for the West at the most propitious moment possible; to have been hired by the *Territorial*

Enterprise on the eve of flush times in Nevada; to have joined the *Quaker City* voyage, the first organized tour of Europe and the Holy Land; to have launched his career as a public speaker with the rise of celebrity culture, when lectures became less instruction and more entertainment; and to have launched a writing career when publishing in the United States became a growth industry. Sam was repeatedly in the right place at the right time. And at least in the way he told the story, he repeatedly escaped death and marriage until middle age by pure chance. I have tried to narrate his story in the most accurate, verifiable, comprehensive, and interesting manner possible, without "stretchers" or whitewash, and with Sam's public mask stripped away.

As usual, I have also depended upon the kindnesses of strangers as well as friends in the compilation of these volumes. I wish to acknowledge in particular the help of Richard Bucci, Victor Fischer, Mandy Gagel, Benjamin Griffin, Robert Hirst, Melissa Martin, Leslie Myrick, Neda Salem, Harriet Elinor Smith, and Bailey Strelow of the Mark Twain Project at the Bancroft Library, University of California–Berkeley; Tim Morgan, Barbara Snedecor, Steve Webb, and Mark Woodhouse of the Center for Mark Twain Studies at Elmira College; Joe Lane, Frances Lopez, Randy Moorehead, and the other staff in the interlibrary loan office of the Zimmerman Library at the University of New Mexico; Dee Dee Lopez of the Department of English at the University of New Mexico; Rebecca Darby of Doe Library, University of California–Berkeley; Jasmine Esterl, Andrea Kratzer, Günter Leypoldt, and David Westley of the Anglistisches Seminar, Universität Heidelberg; and John Bird, Nathan Coleman, Jules Austin Hojnowski, Jerry Loving, Logan MacClyment, Kevin Mac Donnell, Bob Stewart, Gregory Thum, Alan Vetter, Rachelle Weigel, and Harry Wonham. I am also profoundly indebted to Gary Kass, Clair Willcox, Drew Griffith, and Mary S. Conley of the University of Missouri Press, and to copyeditor Brian Bendlin.

Albuquerque, New Mexico
December 28, 2016

Prologue

Bombay, India, January 22, 1896

Sᴀᴍ ᴄʟᴇᴍᴇɴs ᴡᴀs at both the apex of his international celebrity and the nadir of his personal fortunes, almost $100,000 in debt from ill-fated investments at a time when a thousand dollars a year was a comfortable middle-class income, on an arduous lecture tour around the world at the age of sixty to repay his creditors. After Sam checked into Watson's Hotel with his wife Livy and daughter Clara, the "burly German" manager came to their rooms with three servants "to see to arranging things" and deliver their luggage. Sam recorded in his journal what happened next:

> A vast glazed door opening upon a balcony needed opening or closing or cleaning or something. A native went at it; seemed to be doing it well enough; but not to the manager's mind, who didn't *state* that fact or explain where the defect was, but briskly gave him a cuff & *then* an arrogant word of explanation or command. The native took the shameful treatment with meekness, saying nothing, & not showing in his face or manner any resentment.

Sam was stunned. "I had not seen the like of this for 50 years," he observed. He was transported in a flash of memory back to his boyhood in Hannibal, Missouri, and he recalled "the forgotten fact that this was the *usual* way of explaining one's desires to a slave. I was able to remember that the method seemed to me right & natural in those days, I being born to it & unaware that elsewhere there were other methods; but I was also able to remember that those unresented cuffings made me sorry for the victim & ashamed for the punisher." Months later, while writing his final travel book in London, he reflected on the implications of this epiphany:

> For just one second, all that goes to make the me in me was in a Missourian village, on the other side of the globe, vividly seeing again these forgotten pictures of fifty years ago, and wholly unconscious of all things but just those; and in the next second I was back in Bombay, and that kneeling native's smitten cheek was not done tingling yet! Back to boyhood—fifty years; back to age again, another fifty; and a flight equal to the circumference of the globe—all in two seconds by the watch![1]

THE LIFE OF MARK TWAIN
THE EARLY YEARS

CHAPTER 1

Ancestry

He was well born ... and that's worth as much in a man as it is in a horse.

—*Adventures of Huckleberry Finn*

SAMUEL LANGHORNE CLEMENS was descended from a long line of lower-cas(t)e protestants, dissenters, and rapscallions, so it is fair to say that he was to the manner born. According to family tradition, some of his forefathers "were pirates and slavers in Elizabeth's time. But this is no discredit to them," he explained in his autobiography, because piracy was "a respectable trade then" and like his character Tom Sawyer he "had desires to be a pirate myself." Among his ancestors may also have been a certain Gregory Clement, a London merchant, member of Parliament, and one of the judges who in 1649 signed the death warrant for Charles I. Clement was expelled from Parliament three years later for becoming "too publick a Fornicator." After the Restoration in 1660, Gregory Clement went into hiding but was soon discovered, decapitated, and disemboweled, his lands seized and his head displayed on a pike atop Westminster Hall in Charing Cross. Still, Gregory (or Geoffrey, as Sam mistakenly called him) "did what he could toward reducing the list of crowned shams of his day." Sam even noted in his journal in 1890, as if in tribute to his Roundhead kinsman, that the "assassination of a crowned head whenever & wherever opportunity offers should be the first article of all subjects' religion." Unfortunately, while Gregory's son James Clement immigrated to America in 1670, there is no hard evidence that he sired any of Sam's doggedly middle-class and middlebrow ancestors, the Clemenses of Virginia. Sam was nevertheless convinced that "Clement the martyr-maker was an ancestor of mine" and he always regarded the regicide "with favor, and in fact pride."[1]

Sam often boasted that he was descended from English nobility and the First Families of Virginia. As he declared with an assumption of privilege in 1900, "I was born into the leisure class,"[2] and he was not far wrong. The earliest Clemens related to him who is known to have lived in the New World was Samuel B. Clemens, who married Pamela Goggin in Bedford County, Virginia, in 1797. She was the granddaughter of Stephen Goggin, an Anglican who emigrated from Ireland in 1742, and the daughter of Stephen Goggin Jr., who served in the Revolutionary Army and married Rachel Moorman in 1773; a Quaker, she was disowned for marrying outside the faith. After his wedding to Pamela Goggin, Samuel B. Clemens paid a thousand dollars for two slaves, four hundred acres of land near Goose Creek, and a mahogany sideboard, and then went to farming. Their first child, John Marshall Clemens, the father of Samuel Langhorne Clemens, was born in August 1798. Four years after Samuel B. Clemens was killed in a house-raising accident in 1805 his widow married her childhood sweetheart and resettled in Adair County, Kentucky.

When Marshall Clemens reached his majority in 1819, by the laws of primogeniture he inherited three of his father's ten slaves, the mahogany sideboard, and pride in his putative descent from Virginia cavaliers. He was also presented with a bill for almost nine hundred dollars by his stepfather for the expense of raising him and his siblings. He began to study law in the office of the county attorney in Columbia, Kentucky, the seat of Adair County, and earned his license to practice in October 1822. He married Jane Casey Lampton, the mother of Samuel Langhorne Clemens, the following May. Her dowry consisted of three slaves. That is, all four of Sam Clemens's grandparents and both of his parents were slaveholders. Marshall Clemens soon sold one of the slaves Jane brought to the marriage, a seventeen-year-old man named Green, to William Lester of Mississippi for $250. He did not need the cash, but apparently wanted to reduce his household expenses and, from his perspective, was overstocked with inventory. Lester paid him with an IOU.[3]

Jane Clemens's lineage was more distinguished than her husband's, though not as distinguished as she thought. According to family tradition, her paternal grandfather William Lampton immigrated to Virginia with his older brother Samuel around 1740, and Samuel was the legitimate Earl of Durham who had been cheated of his rightful inheritance. As Sam Clemens averred in 1891,

> My mother is descended from the younger of two English brothers named Lambton, who settled in this country a few generations ago. The tradition goes that the elder of the two eventually fell heir to a certain estate in England (now an earldom), and died right away. This has always been the way with our family. They always die when they could make anything by not doing it. The two Lambtons left plenty of Lambtons behind them; and when, at last, about fifty years ago, the English baronetcy was exalted to an earldom, the great tribe of American Lambtons began to bestir themselves—that is, those descended from the elder branch.

Sam's purported cousin Jesse Leathers, the great-grandson of Samuel Lampton, repeatedly tried to prove his claim to the Lambton fortune throughout his life to no avail. Still, it was an endeavor Sam occasionally aided and abetted with gifts of money. Not that he put much stock in the family tradition. Henry Watterson, the longtime editor of the *Louisville Courier-Journal* and Sam's distant relation by marriage, remembered that the two of them "grew up on old wives' tales of estates and titles, which—maybe it was a kindred sense of humor in both of us—we treated with shocking irreverence." In fact, William and Samuel Lampton were descended not from the Earl of Durham but from Mark Lampton, a Maryland tobacco farmer, who established the family line in America.[4]

Despite all the genealogical hairsplitting, Jane Lampton Clemens was in fact distantly related through her father to the genteel Lambtons of Durham and through her mother to an officer in George Washington's army and to Indian fighters who immigrated to Kentucky with Daniel Boone. Born there in 1803, she was the daughter of Benjamin Lampton, a yeoman farmer, dry goods merchant, and slaveholder. As Sam Clemens writes of the family in the fragment "Hellfire Hotchkiss" (1897), "for more than two centuries they have been as good as anybody about them; they have been slave-holding planters, professional men, politicians—now and then a merchant, but never a mechanic. They have always been gentlemen. And they were that in England before they came over."[5]

Jane's courtship by Marshall Clemens was a whirlwind affair. She was by all accounts a beautiful, vivacious Southern belle, an accomplished rider, "the handsomest girl and the wittiest, as well as the best dancer, in all Kentucky," according to Albert Bigelow Paine. After her death in 1890 Jane Clemens was described by her minister as "a woman of the sunniest temperament, lively, affable, a general favorite." Sam idealized her and subscribed to the conventional mid-Victorian ideologies of gender—the cult of true womanhood and the mythology of the "angel in the house"—in his portrayals of her. She had "a large heart; a heart so large that everybody's griefs and everybody's joys found welcome in it and hospitable accommodation," he wrote shortly after her death. "She was of a sunshiny disposition, and her long life was mainly a holiday to her. She always had the heart of a young girl. Through all of the family troubles she maintained a kind of perky stoicism." She once prevented a "vicious devil" from lashing his young daughter by giving him a tongue-lashing of her own, and he eventually "asked her pardon, and gave her his rope." She was a cat lover, according to her son, feeding and caring for nineteen of them in 1845 and inspiring Sam's own lifelong affection for felines. "She never used large words, but she had a natural gift for making small ones do effective work," Sam also remembered. She lived to the age of nearly ninety years "and was capable with her tongue to the last—especially when a meanness or an injustice roused her spirit. She has come handy to me several times in my books," including *The Gilded Age* (1873), his first novel, where she is re-created in Mrs. Hawkins, and *The Adventures of Tom Sawyer* (1876), where she figures as Aunt Polly. His mother, Sam recalled,

> was the most eloquent person whom I have met in all my days, but I did not know it then, and I suppose that no one in all the village suspected that she was a marvel, or indeed that she was in any degree above the common. I had been abroad in the world for twenty years and known and listened to many of its best talkers before it at last dawned upon me that in the matter of moving and pathetic eloquence none of them was the equal of that untrained and art-less talker out there in the western village, that obscure little woman with the beautiful spirit and the great heart and the enchanted tongue.[6]

Unfortunately, she married Marshall Clemens not because she loved him but because she was on the rebound from her first suitor. Richard Ferrel Barrett, a young medical student, began to woo her when she was eighteen. They broke up as the result of a misunderstanding, and she wed Marshall Clemens, a clerk in her uncle's law office, in a pique.

As a result, though their marriage lasted twenty-four years, it was hardly a warm and reverential one. "All through my boyhood," Sam remembered,

> I had noticed that the attitude of my father and mother toward each other was that of courteous, considerate, and always respectful, and even deferen-tial, friends; that they were always kind toward each other, thoughtful of each other, but that there was nothing warmer; there were no outward and visible demonstrations of affection. . . . [T]he absence of exterior demonstration of affection for my mother had no surprise for me. By nature she was warm-hearted, but it seemed to me quite natural that her warm-heartedness should be held in reserve in an atmosphere like my father's.

"Stern" and "austere" were the adjectives Sam used most often over the years to describe his father, sometimes in conjunction with "taciturn," "irritable," "dour," and "humorless." He described the character Judge Carpenter (mod-eled on Marshall Clemens) in his "Villagers of 1840–3" (1897) as a "stern, unsmiling" man who "never demonstrated affection for wife or child." The judge had learned that his wife had married him "to spite another man. Silent, austere, of perfect probity and high principle; ungentle of manner toward his children, but always a gentleman in his phrasing." Similarly, in *Following the Equator* (1897) Sam wrote, "My father was a refined and kindly gentleman, very grave, rather austere, of rigid probity, a sternly just and upright man."

Like Judge Driscoll in *The Tragedy of Pudd'nhead Wilson* (1894), Marshall Clemens was proud of his Virginia ancestry because to "be a gentleman . . . was his only religion." According to a historian in Hannibal, Missouri, he was also known for his "vigorous and scathing pen . . . when he chose to write for the papers," though nothing he published is known to survive. But he was not particularly well-read. Sam noted in 1870 that the only poem his father enjoyed during "the long half century that he lived" was Henry Wadsworth Longfellow's *Hiawatha*.[7] Yet even this claim betrays the flexibility of Sam's memory: his father died in 1847, eight years before *Hiawatha* was published. Marshall Clemens became the model for Judge Thatcher in *Tom Sawyer*, Judge Griswold in the unfinished *Simon Wheeler, Detective* (ca. 1877), and Colonel Grangerford in *Adventures of Huckleberry Finn* (1885).

The year after their marriage, Marshall and Jane Clemens settled in Gainesboro, the seat of Jackson County in east Tennessee, on the Cumberland River, near the homes of one of Jane's cousins and her sister Patsy. This was the first in a series of moves that led nowhere but to misery and destitution. John Adams Quarles, four years younger than Marshall Clemens, married Patsy Lampton in Gainesboro in June 1825. He shared the freethinking ways of his brother-in-law and flirted with such heretical ideas as Universalism. He became Sam's favorite uncle and the model for Uncle Silas Phelps in *Huckleberry Finn*. Much as Sam declares in his autobiography that "I have not come across a better man" than John Quarles, Huck insists that Silas was "the innocentest, best old soul I ever see" and "a mighty nice old man."[8] The Whiggish Clemens, who was named for John Marshall, the Virginian who served as secretary of state and the fourth chief justice of the U.S. Supreme Court, was eager to launch a law practice in Gainesboro. But instead of increasing their income, the Clemenses only increased their expenses with the birth of their first child, Orion, in July 1825.

They soon pulled up stakes and cast their lot forty miles east, in Jamestown, Tennessee, on the Obed River in Fentress County, a region known as "the Knobs." Though Sam never visited the village, he depicted it as Obedstown in *The Gilded Age*. During his first months there, Marshall Clemens reached the pinnacle of his legal career. He opened a small store, practiced law, was elected county commissioner, helped to design and build the county courthouse, served as clerk of the circuit court and occasionally as the acting attorney for Fentress County, and bought thousands of acres of land timbered with virgin yellow pine for little more than one cent per acre. In *The Gilded Age*, Silas Hawkins, the character Sam based on his father, "proudly boasts of its potential to increase in value, saying, 'the whole tract would not sell for over a third of a cent an acre now, but some day people will be glad to get it for twenty dollars, fifty dollars, a hundred dollars an acre!

What would you say to . . . *a thousand dollars an acre.*'" All that was required to maintain title to the land was to "pay the trifling taxes on it yearly—five or ten dollars." The size of the tract, some twenty miles south of Jamestown between the Cumberland and Tennessee Rivers, has been variously estimated: Sam later claimed in his autobiography that his father purchased upwards of seventy-five thousand acres for about four hundred dollars.[9] While the Clemens acreage in Tennessee was substantial, it never amounted to the stupendous tracts cherished in family lore. A more careful and recent examination of the county records reveals that Marshall Clemens actually acquired about twenty-six thousand acres piecemeal over a period of twelve years. Still, who would have imagined that such an asset would become a liability, less a boon than a family curse? The land "influenced our life" for "more than a generation," Sam later complained. "It kept us hoping and hoping during forty years. . . . It put our energies to sleep and made visionaries of us—dreamers and indolent. We were always going to be rich next year—no occasion to work." It was, he noted, "not worth while to go at anything in serious earnest until the land was disposed of and we could embark intelligently in something." As Washington Hawkins, Silas's son, declares in *The Gilded Age*, the land

> began to curse me when I was a baby, and it has cursed every hour of my life to this day. . . . I have chased [fortune] years and years as children chase butterflies. We might all have been prosperous, now; we might all have been happy, all these heart-breaking years, if we had accepted our poverty at first and gone contentedly to work and built up our own wealth by our own toil and sweat.

Unfortunately, Jamestown failed to prosper during the months the Clemens family lived there. As Paine writes, it grew "almost immediately" to a village "of twenty-five houses—mainly log houses—and stopped."[10] There was little need there for the services of a lawyer. The store also failed, and all the while the Clemens clan increased in number, with the births of daughters Pamela in September 1827 and Margaret in May 1830, and a son, Pleasant Hannibal, in 1828 or 1829. Almost nothing is known about this child. He was so frail he lived only about three months, probably because he was born prematurely, perhaps because he was born deformed. His birth is not recorded in the family Bible, an indication he was never christened, and Sam never afterward mentioned this brother he never knew. As Stephen Crane writes of Maggie's baby brother Tommie in *Maggie: A Girl of the Streets* (1893), he simply "went away" in an "insignificant coffin."

The year after Margaret's birth, Marshall Clemens moved his family again, a few miles north to the new settlement of Pall Mall, in the Wolf River valley, where he opened another store and became the postmaster. In

June 1832 the Clemenses became parents for the fourth time with the birth of their son Benjamin. Marshall Clemens eked out a living for a few years, partly by selling five of the six slaves he and Jane had inherited, including a middle-aged handyman or "man of all work" known as Uncle Ned. By the time Marshall and his family fled Fentress County for Missouri in spring 1835 the only slave he still owned was a young domestic named Jenny, who may been a wedding gift to the young couple from Jane's grandmother. By the age of thirty-six, moreover, his health had begun to suffer: he was afflicted with debilitating headaches, and one historian refers vaguely to his "shattered nerves." Squire Hawkins in *The Gilded Age* at a comparable juncture in his life "had a worn look that made him seem older."[11]

What to do but start over again? Spurred in part by the Missouri Compromise, which had opened the territory to slavery and white settlement, Patsy and John Quarles and their many children, as well as Jane and Patsy's father Ben Lampton and their stepmother Diana, had left Kentucky for "the merest little bit of a village" called Florida in Monroe County, Missouri, on the Salt River, a few miles west of the Mississippi. The Clemenses decided to move to Missouri, too. They liquidated their assets in Tennessee—all but the vast land Marshall Clemens believed would eventually establish the family fortune—and, according to Paine, traveled by horse and carriage to Columbia and Louisville and by steamer to St. Louis, where they planned to live. But when they arrived, Jane Clemens explained, they discovered that an outbreak of cholera was raging in the city. So in early June 1835 they pushed on to the "almost invisible village" (as Sam called it) of Florida, where they would at least be welcomed by family. John Quarles had bought a farm four miles from the village and ran it with slave labor. He also kept a store in Florida, which boasted a population of about one hundred, at the intersection of its two streets, "each a couple of hundred yards long." Marshall Clemens accepted his brother-in-law's offer of a partnership in the store, found work as a wagonmaker, and rented a two-room white frame house with a lean-to kitchen on Mill Street near the center of town. Within a month of his arrival in the village he acquired a total of 240 acres of land in the county by purchase or government grant, and in September 1835 he bought a nearly three-acre lot north of town for three hundred dollars on which he planned to build a house.[12] From all indications, Marshall Clemens seemed ready to settle.

CHAPTER 2

The Villages

Human nature cannot be studied in cities except at a disadvantage—a village is the place. There you can know your man inside & out—in a city you but know his crust; & his crust is usually a lie.

—Notebook, ca. 1882

ON NOVEMBER 30, 1835—some seven months after the Clemens family arrived in Florida, Missouri—Jane bore their sixth child, Samuel Langhorne, named for John Marshall Clemens's father and one of his old Virginia friends. Sam's birth increased the population of the hamlet by 1 percent, he would later brag. He was born into genteel poverty two months prematurely; that is, he was likely conceived during his parents' trek west from Tennessee. He was a Southron by both birth and upbringing. Contrary to the claims of Monroe County historians and despite its preservation in a visitors' center on the banks of Mark Twain Lake near the village of Florida, Samuel Langhorne Clemens was probably not born in the house on Mill Street where the family resided—Jane Clemens insisted that "it was too small" for her accouchement—but in the nearby log home of Ben Lampton, the patriarch of the clan, on Main Street. Six months later, Marshall bought this house for $1,050 and moved his family into it. Years later, ironically, it was converted into the first church in Florida and eventually fell into decay and was torn down around the turn of the twentieth century. Thus, the rustic cabin enshrined in the visitors' center may be the house where Sam lived as a child, but it is not the house where he was born. In any case, his mother remembered, when she first saw him "I could see no promise in him. But I felt it my duty to do the best I could. To raise him if I could." The scrawny baby barely survived the winter. His prospects were not encouraging. In fact, he remembered in 1890, he "was sick the first seven years" of his life and subsisted "on expensive allopathic medicines." Jane Clemens, a homeopath and hydrotherapist, alternately dosed him with castor and cod liver oil and doused him with water. Over fifty years later, she admitted to her famous son that "at first I was afraid you would die"—then after "a slight, reflective pause" she added, "and after that I was afraid you wouldn't."[1]

◆

As had been the case in the Knobs, John Marshall Clemens's future in Florida seemed promising at first; he became a trustee of the new Florida Academy and began to practice law again. In November 1837 he took the oath of office as a judge of the Monroe County Court and for the rest of his life he was known as Judge Clemens. A county judge was "the position of highest dignity in the gift of the ballot," Sam reflected in 1897, and he characterized Judge Thatcher in *The Adventures of Tom Sawyer* (1876) with only a hint of irony as "a prodigious personage" and "most august creation." Marshall Clemens dissolved his partnership with John Quarles and opened his own mercantile store across the street, and he was locally esteemed as a well-born descendant of the First Families of Virginia. As his son Sam would explain in *The Tragedy of Pudd'nhead Wilson* (1894), in Missouri "a recognized superiority attached to any person who hailed from Old Virginia; and this superiority was exalted to supremacy when a person of such nativity could also prove descent from the First Families of that great commonwealth." An advocate of internal improvements and a supporter of the political agenda of Henry Clay, Marshall lobbied state authorities to select Florida as the seat of Monroe County and the federal government to authorize the bonds necessary to dredge the Salt River and construct a series of dams and locks to enable steamboats to navigate it. The scheme inspired Sam's satirical reference to the fraudulent Columbus River Slackwater Navigation Company in *The Gilded Age* (1873). Marshall Clemens also hoped that a railroad might be built between Florida and Paris, Missouri, twelve miles away. He built a four-room house—actually a pair of two-room cabins—for the family on the homestead site he had acquired north of town.

By 1837 the village was growing rapidly, with three mills and four distilleries. According to Margaret Sanborn, the distilleries annually produced some "ten thousand gallons of whisky and three thousand gallons of brandy and gin."[2]

Then all went to smash in the credit crunch and long economic depression that followed the Panic of 1837.[3] John Quarles wrote his brother from Florida, Missouri, in August 1838 that "times are very hard in this State" and that "the Merchants are breaking on every hand." Marshall Clemens's store failed because he could no longer buy inventory on credit in St. Louis. Neither the dredging project nor the railroad was financed, nor was Florida named the county seat. The village was doomed; today it is uninhabited. The seventh and last of the Clemens children, son Henry, was born there on July 13, 1838. A year later their daughter Margaret died within a week of contracting "bilious" or yellow fever. She had been "in disposition & manner

Figure 1. The Clemens homestead in Florida, Missouri, ca. 1890. Photograph by E. B. and C. M. Lasley. Courtesy of the Library of Congress.

like Sam full of life," Jane Clemens later wrote, but after she fell ill she "never was in her right mind 3 minutes at a time."[4]

With a wife and five surviving children, Marshall Clemens rolled the dice again. In mid-November 1839, two weeks before Sam's fourth birthday and three months after Margaret's death, he sold his real estate holdings in Monroe County, including his homestead north of town, to a land speculator named Ira Stout for $5,000 and bought from him a quarter of a city block, about nine thousand square feet of property with a hotel on it, in Hannibal, Missouri, thirty miles to the east, on the Mississippi River, for $7,000 in gold. He borrowed $250 for the down payment from his distant cousin James Clemens Jr. (a prosperous St. Louis lawyer, merchant, and one of the directors of the Phoenix Insurance Company, headquartered in St. Louis) and nearly $750 from Jane's half brother James Andrew Hays Lampton, aka Uncle Jim, who had also settled near Florida with his family.[5] James A. H. Lampton had been trained as a doctor at McDowell's Medical College in St. Louis but was sickened by the sight of blood—an occupational hazard for a physician.

Located in the hollow between Holliday's Hill to the north and Lover's Leap to the south, founded by refugees from the New Madrid earthquakes of 1811–12 and named for the defeated Carthaginian general, Hannibal was little more than a one-horse hamlet in 1840, with a cigar factory, a tobacco warehouse, and a weekly newspaper. W. D. Howells once described it as a "loafing, out-at-elbows, down-at-the-heels, slaveholding Mississippi River town," but within a couple of years it boasted four general stores, three sawmills, two planing mills, three blacksmith forges, two hotels, three saloons, two churches, a hemp factory, and a distillery. Its pork-packing plants, where some ten thousand hogs were slaughtered every fall and winter, were located on the south side of Bear Creek, which flowed eastward through the center of town before emptying into the Mississippi. Marshall Clemens moved his family into the Virginia House, the hotel he had acquired at the corner of Hill and Main Streets, and opened a store on the premises stocked with inventory he was allowed to buy on credit in St. Louis, some fourteen hours downriver by steamboat. Fifteen-year-old Orion worked in the store and seven-year-old Ben was enrolled in a boys' academy. Twelve-year-old Pamela and four-year-old Sam attended a dame school on Main Street run by Elizabeth Horr, wife of the town cooper and a New England lady of middle age, who charged twenty-five cents per week per student for instruction. Whereas Pamela was commended by the teacher in November 1840 for her "amiable deportment and faithful application to her various studies," Sam claimed later that he was switched for misbehavior on his first day of class. He remembered, too, that Lizzie Horr always began the day "with prayer and a chapter from the New Testament."[6]

For a few months, all was well. As Sam later wrote in his essay "Villagers of 1840–3" (1897), his father was "still a small storekeeper—but progressing." After more than a decade of tribulation, he seemed finally to have landed on his feet. Enter Ira Stout in the role of serpent in this tale of woe. The surviving records are not entirely clear, but Stout apparently bought a consignment of merchandise from Marshall Clemens's store in the fall of 1840 and then either declared bankruptcy or simply refused to pay the debt. In either case, Sam's father was unable to pay for the stock in his store and his store failed in the fall of 1841. On October 13, he was forced to surrender his Hannibal property, including the Virginia House, to James Kerr, the St. Louis merchant who had fronted him the money to buy his inventory. Kerr repossessed, Orion recalled in 1894, "all the dry goods, groceries, boots and shoes and hardware" in the store. Marshall Clemens even offered "his cow and the knives and forks from his table," but Kerr "told him to keep these." When the property was sold in 1843 on behalf of Marshall's creditors, the price was less than four thousand dollars, a sum that later persuaded Sam that Stout had taken advantage of the bankruptcy law to ruin his father—an action that "made a pauper of him." Dixon Wecter, who researched the early history of Hannibal exhaustively, concluded that Stout was "clearly a dead beat" who became enmeshed in "a web of litigation" with several Hannibal citizens, some of whom sued him successfully for failing to pay his debts. In 1847 Stout sold off his holdings in Marion County, including a large house, seven lots on Main Street, and forty acres of timberland and pasture. In 1850 he moved to Quincy, Illinois, twelve miles upriver from Hannibal, but in 1858 he was literally hoist by his own petard: after his conviction in Rochester, New York, on a charge of murder, he was hanged.[7]

Marshall Clemens desperately tried to reverse his slow spiral into destitution in the winter of 1841–42. He apprenticed Orion to the owner of the *Hannibal Journal*, which like the sale of the slave Green in 1825 at least reduced his expenses. "I do not know yet what I can commence at for a business in the spring," he lamented to Jane Clemens in January 1842. "The future taking its complexion from the state of my health of mind, is alternatively beaming in sunshine, or overshadowed with clouds; but mostly cloudy, as you will readily suppose."[8] In a vain attempt to keep the wolf at bay, Marshall traveled to Mississippi in December and to Tennessee and Kentucky in the spring to scrounge for money and, while en route, to sell an aged slave named Charley. He had been given Charley in November 1840 in payment of a bill, but he soon discovered that the slave was so old he was almost worthless. He was offered fifty dollars for Charley in New Orleans and forty dollars in Vicksburg, Mississippi,[9] and eventually traded him in Natchez, Mississippi, for ten barrels of tar worth forty dollars.

The terms of this particular transaction are charged with irony. In an early draft of the novel that became *Pudd'nhead Wilson*, one of the leading characters takes a similar journey to sell a slave and collect a debt. "It never occurred to him," Sam writes, that the slave "had a heart in his bosom to break, & left hearts behind him that could break also." Sam's father was just as oblivious to Charley's plight, but even more so: forty years later, when Sam returned to the river to gather material for his book *Life on the Mississippi* (1883), he belittled the town of Natchez, where his father had sold Charley and where he had often landed during his piloting career. He recalled in chapter 39 its "desperate reputation, morally" in those days and added that it "has not changed notably." It was "still small, straggling, and shabby," with "plenty of drinking, carousing, fisticuffing, and killing there, among the riff-raff of the river."[10]

Moreover, the number forty, the dollar equivalent in tar for which Marshall Clemens traded Charley, is numerically significant in Sam's writing, perhaps for biblical reasons. Noah suffered a flood lasting forty days and nights, and the first Nevada territorial legislature in the winter of 1861, over which Orion Clemens presided (with Sam's assistance), debated a deluge of laws in a session that lasted forty days and nights. The children of Israel wandered in a desert beyond the Mountains of Moab for forty years, and as it so happened the Nevada miners crossing from Virginia City and Carson City to the silver fields in the Humboldt district—including Sam, in 1861—crossed Forty Mile Desert. In 1864 Sam was hired by the San Francisco *Morning Call* at a salary of forty dollars per week, and in "The Celebrated Jumping Frog of Calaveras County" (1865) Jim Smiley and a stranger wager forty dollars on the length of frogs' leaps. The martyred Christ descends to hell for forty days and nights, and in *Adventures of Huckleberry Finn* (1885) a pair of slave hunters who nearly capture Jim instead give Huck two twenty-dollar gold pieces, the king later sells Jim back into slavery for forty dollars, and Tom Sawyer pays Jim forty dollars "for being prisoner for us so patient." If Judas's reward for betraying Christ was thirty pieces of silver, the cost of submitting to slavery and other forms of humiliation in Sam's world (e.g., the purchase price of a slave, a freedman's payment for acting like a slave, the amount of a lost bet to a stranger who fills a frog with quail shot, the weekly salary paid a reporter for drudge work) is forty dollars—exactly the same amount in value that Marshall Clemens received for Charley. Forty is also the number of thieves who conspire to deny Ali Baba a fortune in gold in the *Arabian Nights' Entertainment*, one of Sam's favorite books.[11]

In Vicksburg Marshall Clemens presented William Lester with the unpaid IOU he had received in exchange for Green almost twenty years earlier. With interest, the debt had almost doubled, from $250 to $470. But Lester pled poverty and Clemens relented. "It seemed so very hard upon him [in] these hard times to pay such a sum that I could not have the conscience to hold him to it," he wrote Jane. He agreed to take Lester's note, "payable 1st March next for $250"—that is, for the original amount of the debt, with all interest forgiven—"and let him off at that." He could not squeeze blood money from a turnip. Lester "had no money on hand and I could not get it. Everyone I enquired of said he was entirely solvent and good for it." He planned to sell some of the Tennessee land "and then return to see Lester about the time the note falls due." On this occasion he failed to sell any of it. He spent the remainder of the winter in Kentucky with his mother before returning to Hannibal in the spring via Louisville with a side trip to Vicksburg in another failed attempt to collect the debt Lester owed him. He was still trying to collect the money as late as November 1844,[12] and there is no evidence he ever succeeded.

He arrived back in Hannibal empty-handed and two hundred dollars poorer for the expense of the trip. Orion remembered in his autobiography, which was available to Albert Bigelow Paine but has since been lost, how his mother chided her husband for his failure. Marshall Clemens replied that, as a gentleman, "I cannot dig in the streets." Orion added, "I can see yet the hopeless expression of his face." To make matters worse, in May 1842, the month after Marshall Clemens returned to Hannibal, nine-year-old Ben Clemens fell ill and died within a week. He was the third of Sam's siblings to die before the age of ten, and the only kiss Sam ever saw his parents exchange was beside Ben's deathbed. Jane Clemens "made the children feel the cheek of the dead boy" so that they would "understand the calamity that had befallen" the family—or so Sam remembered later. It was one of his earliest memories. According to the most reliable mortality statistics, the death of a child was an all too common event in Hannibal in the mid-nineteenth century. A quarter of the children in the town died before the age of one, and half of the others died before attaining their majority.[13]

By the end of 1842, with his apprenticeship in Hannibal completed, Orion gravitated to St. Louis and went to work in Thomas Watt Ustick's print shop, sending a few dollars home to his parents. Marshall Clemens was still so poverty-stricken that he was compelled to sell Jenny, his only remaining slave and virtually his only asset, for five hundred dollars.[14] At her request, he offered her to the most benign of the three local slave traders, William Beebe—who promptly sold her down the river. Sam remembered that her sale was "a sore trial, for the woman was almost like one of the family." Years later Jenny resurfaced as a chambermaid on a Mississippi steamboat, like the character Roxy in *Pudd'nhead Wilson*, and "cried and lamented" her fate. She may have been forced to turn to prostitution to survive.[15] Meanwhile, Beebe failed to pay for her, so Marshall Clemens sued him and was awarded damages consisting of "some tin plates, sacks of salt, a screw press, some barrels, and a nine-year-old Negro girl" whom he sold at auction the following year.[16]

Slavery, the "peculiar institution," was woven like raw cotton into the social fabric of Marion County. Largely settled by emigrants from other slave states, it was known as the South Carolina of Missouri for its Southern sympathies. According to the 1840 census it boasted a population of about 10,000, including over 7,000 whites, a few dozen free blacks, and about 2,300 slaves. A decade later, the slave population had increased to about 2,850, and Terrell Dempsey estimates that 44 percent of all white families in the county owned at least one slave. Even Laura Hawkins, the model for Becky Thatcher, the epitome of childhood innocence in *The Adventures of Tom Sawyer*, was a slaveholder. While Sam never witnessed a slave sale, he observed slaves with "the saddest faces I ever saw" lying in chains on the Hannibal dock awaiting

shipment down the river. For the record, moreover, 16 percent of the slaves
in Hannibal in 1860 were of mixed race—irrefutable evidence of the sexual
exploitation of black women by their white masters. Sam remembered later
that "the wise, the good, and the holy" Christian ministers in Hannibal "were
unanimous in the belief that slavery was right, righteous, sacred, the peculiar
pet of the Deity, and a condition which the slave himself ought to be daily and
nightly thankful for." At the time, he certainly shared the racist assumptions
of the adults. In 1852, at the age of sixteen, he referred in his brother's newspaper to the "fat, lazy 'niggers'" who "begin to sweat and look greasy" in warm
weather. As he wrote in the winter of 1897,

> In my schoolboy days I had no aversion to slavery. I was not aware that there
> was anything wrong about it. No one arraigned it in my hearing; the local
> papers said nothing against it; the local pulpit taught us that God approved it,
> that it was a holy thing, and that the doubter need only look in the Bible if he
> wished to settle his mind—and then the texts were read aloud to us to make
> the matter sure; if the slaves themselves had an aversion to slavery, they were
> wise and said nothing.

But there were dissenting voices. A Hannibal chapter of the American Colonization Society was established in June 1847. The Reverend David Nelson,
who had founded the First Presbyterian Church in Hannibal, which Jane
and her children attended, was expelled for his opposition to slavery. He
later established the antislavery Presbyterian Mission Institute in nearby
free-soil Quincy, Illinois. The Reverend Joseph L. Bennett, Nelson's succes-
sor, later became a convert to abolitionism. Given its location a mile across
the river from Illinois, Hannibal was also a clandestine stop on the Underground Railroad.[17]

To be sure, there was little public sympathy for the antislavery cause. "In
that day," as Clemens recalled in 1894, "for a man to speak out openly and
proclaim himself an enemy of negro slavery was simply to proclaim himself a
madman. For he was blaspheming against the holiest thing known to a Mis-
sourian, and could *not* be in his right mind." A case in point was the summer
of 1841 trial in Palmyra, the Marion County seat, of three abolitionists from
Quincy charged with grand theft for inciting three slaves to escape across
the Mississippi River to Illinois and thence to freedom in Canada. (Slaves
were considered "contraband," and the joke went around that abolitionists
were "contra-bandits.") The slaves were allowed to testify for the prosecution, despite a law prohibiting the testimony of blacks against whites. The
case attracted national attention, with reports of it in the St. Louis *Missouri Republican* reprinted in newspapers from New Orleans, Charleston,
and Washington to Philadelphia and Boston, including the *Liberator*, the

antislavery paper edited by William Lloyd Garrison. Marshall Clemens served on the circuit court jury of twelve men who voted to convict the abolitionists, each of whom was sentenced to twelve years of hard labor in the Missouri State Penitentiary at Jefferson City, also known as "the bloodiest 47 acres in America." The case supplied the premise of Sam's unfinished novel "Tom Sawyer's Conspiracy," written in 1897 and narrated by Huck Finn, about a group of rumored "ablitionists laying for a chance to run off some of our niggers to freedom." Sam caricatured William Beebe in the story as Bat Bradish, a cruel slave trader and "the orneriest hound in town," and later as Henry Bascom's father, who was "unloved" but "respected for his muscle and his temper," in the unfinished "Schoolhouse Hill" version of *The Mysterious Stranger*, written between 1897 and 1908.[18]

A month after the trial concluded, Marshall Clemens surrendered all his property to his creditors. Yet in the fall of 1844 the voters of Marion County elected him a justice of the peace. Sam thought, or so he wrote in *Life on the Mississippi*, that his father in this august office "possessed the power of life and death over all men and could hang anybody that offended him." In fact, the job provided a meager income, barely adequate to provide for his family, and required him to enforce the local ordinances regarding slaves and free blacks. Specifically, no freedman could live in Hannibal without a license; any unlicensed black person without proof of freedom could be arrested and jailed as a runaway slave; any black person on the streets of the village after nine in the evening without a pass was subject to a fine; and blacks were not allowed to assemble at night without permission from the mayor. As justice of the peace, Marshall once found a slave guilty of insolence and ordered him "to receive twenty lashes at the hands of the constable." Though Sam asserted in 1885 that he had once heard his father say that "slavery was a great wrong" and that he would have freed Jenny "if he could think it right to give away the property of the family when he was so straitened in means," this memory seems to be what Dixon Wecter calls an "act of filial whitewashing."[19] Even after Marshall sold Jenny he continued to lease slaves.

In fact, he was never one to spare the rod and spoil the child, especially a slave child. He was known locally as "a severe disciplinarian." That is, Sam grew up in a home over which the specter of physical punishment always loomed. Orion bitterly remembered as late as 1873 the frequency of "my father's reprimands," and on his part Sam recalled, "My father and I were always on the most distant terms when I was a boy—a sort of armed neutrality, so to speak. At irregular intervals this neutrality was broken, and suffering ensued; but I will be candid enough to say that the breaking and the suffering were always divided up with strict impartiality between us— which is to say, my father did the breaking, and I did the suffering."[20] Years

later he joked, "I somehow didn't like being round him when I'd done anything he disapproved of," as when Sam stowed away on a steamboat. He
was discovered before the boat landed in Louisiana, Missouri, twenty-five
miles downriver. "I was sent home by some friends of my father's," he later
explained, and his father "met me on my return." Years later, in a magnan-
imous mood, Sam claimed that his father had "laid his hand upon me in
punishment only twice in his life"—once presumably for hiding on the boat,
the other time for telling him a lie—"which surprised me, and showed me
how unsuspicious he was, for that was not my maiden effort. He punished
me those two times only, and never any other member of the family at all; yet
every now and then he cuffed our harmless [leased] slave boy . . . for trifling
little blunders and awkwardnesses."[21]

In the manuscript of this reminiscence Sam had originally written
"lashed" instead of "cuffed," but when his wife Olivia read the manuscript
she glossed in the margin, "I hate to have your father pictured as lashing a
slave boy." Sam responded by changing the word: "it's out, and my father is
whitewashed." But the revision could not obscure the fact that Marshall Clemens was a stern master. On another occasion, after Jenny grabbed a whip
from the threatening hand of Jane Clemens, he punished her by binding her
wrists with a bridle rein and flogging her with a cowhide. Sam explained
that his father "had passed his life among slaves from his cradle" and "acted
from the custom of the time, not his nature." As Arthur G. Pettit adds, "For
a man who thought slave cruelties in Missouri were rare, [Sam] remembered
quite a few of them."[22]

In 1843, seven-year-old Sam Clemens spent the first of five summers with
his mother, sister Pamela, and brother Henry at Patsy and John Quarles's
farm northwest of Florida. Soon after Marshall Clemens left Florida in despair, Uncle John had bought an additional 230 acres of farmland four miles
from the village and built a two-story, four-room log house. The Quarles's
farm became the model for the Phelps farm in *Adventures of Huckleberry
Finn* and *Tom Sawyer, Detective* (1896), as well as a homestead in the fragment "Tupperville-Dobbsville" (ca. 1876–80). As Huck describes it, it was

one of these little one-horse cotton plantations, and they all look alike. A rail
fence round a two-acre yard; a stile made out of logs sawed off and up-ended
in steps, like barrels of a different length, to climb over the fence with, and for
the women to stand on when they are going to jump on to a horse; some sickly
grass-patches in the big yard, but mostly it was bare and smooth, like an old
hat with the nap rubbed off; big double log-house for the white folks—hewed
logs, with the chinks stopped up with mud or mortar, and these mud-stripes
been whitewashed some time or another; round-log kitchen, with a big broad,

open but roofed passage joining it to the house; log smoke-house back of the kitchen; three little log nigger-cabins in a row t'other side the smoke-house; one little hut all by itself away down against the back fence, and some out-buildings down a piece the other side; ash-hopper and big kettle to bile soap in by the little hut; bench by the kitchen door, with bucket of water and a gourd; hound asleep there in the sun; more hounds asleep round about; about three shade trees away off in a corner; some currant bushes and gooseberry bushes in one place by the fence; outside of the fence a garden and a watermel-on patch; then the cotton fields begins, and after the fields the woods.

The farm "was a heavenly place for a boy," Sam remembered in his autobiography.[23]

There slavery existed in perhaps its most benign form. His aunt and uncle apparently never sold a slave, and Sam insisted in later years that he never saw one "misused" on their farm. According to census records, they owned six slaves in 1840 and eleven in 1850, including Aunt Hannah, "a bedrid-den white-headed slave woman whom we visited daily and looked upon with awe," and Uncle Dan'l, the original of Uncle Dan'l in *The Gilded Age*, Dan'l in *The American Claimant* (1892), and Jim in *Huck Finn* and several Tom/Huck sequels. Sam allowed in his autobiography that he had "staged him in books under his own name and as 'Jim,' and carted him all around—to Hannibal, down the Mississippi on a raft, and even across the Desert of Sa-hara in a balloon" in *Tom Sawyer Abroad*. Sam remembered to the end of his life the evenings he spent in the slave quarters on the farm with his Quarles and Lampton cousins and the slave children. He heard from Uncle Dan'l the story "The Golden Arm," which years later he sometimes performed on-stage. He learned, too, the Negro spirituals that he often sang for his family in later years. From these songs he gleaned the impression, as he reminisced in *The Innocents Abroad* (1869), "that the river Jordan was four thousand miles long and thirty-five miles wide." In 1881 he reminisced in a letter to Joel Chandler Harris about the "impressive pauses and eloquent silences" in Uncle Dan'l's delivery,[24] and he remembered in 1907 "the look of Uncle Dan'l's kitchen as it was on privileged nights when I was a child and I can see the white and black children grouped on the hearth, with the firelight playing on their faces and the shadows flickering upon the walls, clear back toward the cavernous gloom of the rear, and I can hear Uncle Dan'l telling the immortal tales."[25] At the Phelps farm, too, Sam "gradually absorbed" the "different dialects" spoken by the slaves, "who had been drawn from two or three States." He would exhibit his gift for dialect thirty years later by re-creating seven nuanced ones in *Huck Finn*.[26]

The color line was not entirely erased there, however. Given the strict so-cial customs of the time, Sam could mingle with slaves more readily and informally on the farm than in the village. But the white children alone attended a country school three miles away once or twice a week in the summer, and even as a child Sam intuited a difference between white and black: "We were comrades and yet not comrades; color and condition interposed a subtle line which both parties were conscious of and which rendered complete fusion impossible." Still, "it was on the farm that I got my strong liking" for the African race "and my appreciation of certain of its fine qualities," he remarked in his autobiography. "This feeling and this estimate have stood the test of sixty years and more, and have suffered no impairment. The black face is as welcome to me now as it was then."[27] Unfortunately, he overstated his lack of racial prejudice; in fact, he harbored some biases for the rest of his life. He may have been a nineteenth-century progressive on issues of race, but Sam was nevertheless more a creature of his own time than of ours.

Back in Hannibal in the fall of 1843 young Sam was exposed for the first time to the murderous violence that was all too common in frontier towns. On September 4, a local farmer named James McFarland was stabbed through the heart in a bar brawl and died an hour later; it was the first recorded murder in the history of Hannibal. McFarland's body was carried to Marshall Clemens's office to await an inquest because, as justice of the peace, Sam's father doubled as the local coroner. As Sam remembered later, he played hooky that day and, to delay the inevitable whipping at home, he crawled in a window of his father's office to hide. In the moonlight he saw the body and leaped out the window to escape the horror. "When I reached home, they whipped me," he added, "but I enjoyed it" compared to the trauma he had suffered. He "slept in the same room" with McFarland's body in nightmares for years to come.[28] The story, first recounted in *The Innocents Abroad*, became a staple in his stage repertoire.

The nightmares became part of a larger pattern of sleep disorders he suffered his entire life. According to one of his Quarles cousins, even as a child Sam "was a victim of somnambulism" or sleepwalking "and a close watch had to be kept on him to keep him from meeting with some mishap." He interrupted the comic narrative of *The Innocents Abroad* to allude, quite unexpectedly, to the night terrors he endured on the "pleasure excursion" to Europe and the Holy Land in 1867: "to bed, with drowsy brains harassed with a mad panorama that mixes up pictures of France, of Italy, of the ship, of the ocean, of home, in grotesque and bewildering disorder. Then a melting away of familiar faces, of cities, and of tossing waves, into a great calm of forgetfulness and peace. After which, the nightmare." The reference anticipates similar nightmares suffered by characters in *The Prince and the Pauper* ("Troublous dreams, troublous dreams!"), *Pudd'nhead Wilson* ("Now what was that dream?"), and other works. "With the going down of the sun my faith failed, and the clammy fears gathered about my heart," he wrote in his autobiography. "In my age, as in my youth, night brings me many a deep remorse." From "the cradle up," he confessed, he had never been "quite sane in the night."[29]

Two years after McFarland's death, Sam was privy to the first premeditated murder in Hannibal history. Around noon on January 24, 1845, William Perry Owsley, a merchant and slave trader, killed Sam Smarr of rural Marion County. According to testimony at the trial, Smarr thought Owsley had cheated one of his friends, and he publicly vilified Owsley for several weeks. Owsley confronted him at the corner of Hill and Main Streets, mere feet from the Clemens house, and shot him twice in the chest at point-blank range. A witness testified that after Smarr fell, Owsley turned and walked away. Smarr was carried into Grant's Drug Store, where he died a half hour later. Sam was among the crowd of villagers who watched him breathe his last. As with the corpse of James McFarland, the death of "poor Smarr," Sam remembered,

> supplied me with dreams and in them I always saw again the grotesque closing picture—the great family Bible spread open upon the profane old man's breast by some thoughtful idiot . . . adding the torture of its leaden weight to the dying struggles. We are curiously made. In all that throng of gaping and sympathetic onlookers there was not one with common sense enough to perceive that an anvil would have been in better taste there than the Bible, less open to sarcastic criticism and swifter in its atrocious work. In my nightmares I gasped and struggled for breath under the crush of that vast book for many a night.

He dramatized the incident in chapters 21 and 22 of *Adventures of Huckleberry Finn*, in which Colonel Sherburn shoots the drunken Boggs in cold blood. In 1900, Sam wrote a friend that he could not "ever forget Boggs, because I saw him die, with a family Bible spread open on his breast. . . . Boggs represents Smarr in the book." In fact, Owsley was arrested for murder, and like Sherburn he seems to have defied a lynch mob. In "The United States of Lyncherdom" (written in 1901), Sam remembered that as a boy he "saw a brave gentleman deride" a clique of vigilantes intent on hanging him. That is, in Sam's imagination Sherburn is an ambiguous figure who both murders an innocent drunk and then boldly taunts a masked throng modeled on the Ku Klux Klan. In any case, as justice of the peace Marshall Clemens was able to turn the gunplay to his advantage. He was paid over fifteen dollars by the county for transcribing legal documents and deposing witnesses.[30] Owsley was acquitted at his murder trial in March, but "there was a cloud upon him—a social chill," Sam remembered. Owsley sold his store on Main Street in May 1849 and emigrated to the gold fields in California the next month, though he returned to Hannibal in 1852. In early March of that year he defaulted on a debt and on March 17 a slave woman he owned hanged herself, apparently because he planned to sell her. The two lots he had put up as collateral on the loan were sold at auction on April 17. Owsley was still buying and selling slaves in Hannibal as late as April 1853.[31]

There are three more instances of Sam's exposure to violence when he was a child. In about 1845, not long after witnessing Smarr's death, he watched as two young men tried to murder their uncle. One of them held the victim to the ground while the other tried to shoot him with an Allen revolver that repeatedly misfired. The next year, when he was ten (or so he claimed in 1897), he watched in horror as an angry white man flung "a lump of iron-ore" at a leased slave merely for "doing something awkwardly—as if that were a crime." It crushed the skull of the black man, who died within the hour. Sam conceded that the white man "had a right to kill his slave if he wanted to, and yet it seemed a pitiful thing & somehow wrong." Nobody in Hannibal "approved of that murder," he added, and the citizens felt "considerable sympathy" for the slave's owner, "who had been bereft of valuable property by a worthless person who was not able to pay for it," but "no one said much about it." And in August 1847, while swimming and boating with his friends John Briggs and the Bowen brothers on the Mississippi near Sny Island, across from Hannibal on the Illinois side of the river in free territory, he saw the bloated and mutilated body of a fugitive slave named Neriam Todd surface from its underwater grave. Todd had escaped to Illinois, where Bence Blankenship, oldest son of the town drunk, found and fed him instead of reporting him to the authorities and claiming a reward. Eventually Todd was discovered by some woodcutters, who chased him into the swamp where he died, either by drowning or lynching. His body was "much mutilated" when it was recovered.[32]

Late in 1843 the Clemens family moved out of the Virginia House and into a small home next door. James Kerr had sold the building lot, about twenty feet in width, to James Clemens Jr. in late October for $330, and Marshall Clemens leased the land from his well-to-do cousin for $28 a year and built on it a white clapboard house, the "Mark Twain Boyhood Home" that attracts tourists to Hannibal to this day.[33]

What Sam only half facetiously later called "the turning point of my life"—an outbreak of measles in Hannibal—occurred in the spring of 1844. Nearly forty people died, including seven in one day. Sam remembered, accurately enough, that

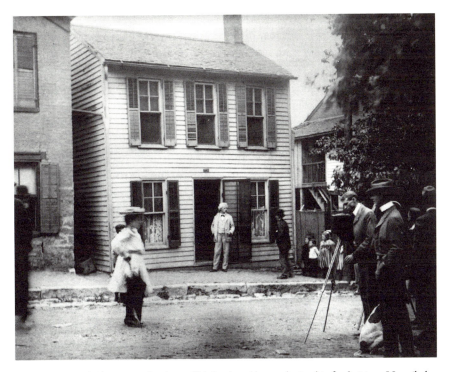

Figure 2. Samuel Clemens at the door of his boyhood home during his final visit to Hannibal in 1902. Collection of Gary Scharnhorst.

for a time a child died almost every day. The village was paralyzed with fright, distress, despair. Children that were not smitten with the disease were imprisoned in their homes to save them from the infection. In the homes there were no cheerful faces, there was no music, there was no singing but of solemn hymns, no voice but of prayer, no romping was allowed, no noise, no laughter, the family moved spectrally about on tiptoe, in a ghostly hush. I was a prisoner. My soul was steeped in this awful dreariness—and in fear. At some time or other every day and every night a sudden shiver shook me to the marrow, and I said to myself, "There, I've got it! and I shall die." Life on these miserable terms was not worth living, and at last I made up my mind to get the disease and have it over, one way or the other.

His best friend Will Bowen was bedridden with the illness, which was as contagious as laughter, and Sam snuck into the Bowen house and climbed into bed with him. By the time he was discovered, he was infected, and he was sick for two weeks. But the measles "were not what I expected they would be," he told an interviewer in 1902; the disease "brought me within a shade of death's door."[34] He put the incident to good use later in "Tom

Sawyer's Conspiracy" (1897–1902), in which Tom contracts the measles from his friend Joe Harper exactly as Sam contracted them from Will.

Jane Clemens treated Sam with castor oil and hot salt water with mustard and pressed socks full of hot ashes to his chest, though he "was too weak and miserable to care much." She also inflicted the water cure on him. As he testified before a New York State legislative committee on public health in 1901, "I remember how my mother used to stand me up naked in the back-yard every morning and throw buckets of cold water on me. . . . And then, when the dousing was over, she would wrap me up in a sheet wet with ice wa-ter and then wrap blankets around that and put me into bed. . . . I would get up a perspiration that was something worth seeing." Sam reconstructed the experience both in the abandoned early version of *Tom Sawyer* that Paine ti-tled "Boy's Manuscript" (written circa 1868) and in *Tom Sawyer*: Aunt Polly herded Tom "out at daylight every morning, stood him up in the wood-shed and drowned him with a deluge of cold water; then she scrubbed him down with a towel like a file, and so brought him to; then she rolled him up in a wet sheet and put him away under blankets till she sweated his soul clean and 'the yellow stains of it came through his pores.'" Despite this treatment, Sam recovered. He claimed later that had he not contracted the measles, his mother would not have allowed him to drop out of school or apprenticed him to a printer—thus the disease was the first in a chain of events that led inexorably to his literary career. Or, as he joked in 1901, he joined the liter-ary profession "because I had the measles."[35]

During the two weeks that Tom Sawyer is ill, as Sam wrote in the novel chronicling Tom's adventures, "a melancholy change" came "over everything and every creature" because "there had been a 'revival,' and everybody had 'got religion.'" Within another two weeks, however, the villagers suffered a "relapse" and backslid into their sinful ways. In the 1840s and 1850s Han-nibal was in fact a welter of millennial and evangelical zeal. On the evening of October 22, 1844, Sam watched as the local Millerites, believers in the prophecy of William Miller that the Second Coming of Christ would occur that night, climbed Holliday's Hill (Cardiff Hill, in *Tom Sawyer*) to await the end of the world. The appearance in March 1843 of the most brilliant comet of the century had been hailed by some enthusiastic Millerites as an omen from heaven, a last warning that corroborated the calculations of their prophet. To judge from his occasional references to them in his writings, the Millerites made a lasting impression on Sam, though he was barely eight years old at the time. In *The Innocents Abroad*, for example, he explained how "twenty-five years ago a multitude of people in America put on their ascension robes, took a tearful leave of their friends, and made ready to fly up into heaven at the first blast of the trumpet. But the angel did not blow it. Miller's resurrection day was a failure. The Millerites were disgusted."[36]

Religious rivalries in Hannibal were often contentious, to be sure. When Melicent Holliday quit or "withdrew from the jurisdiction" of the local Episcopal church in April 1853, she wrote a card to that effect for publication in the *Hannibal Journal*. Marshall Clemens "attended no church and never spoke of religious matters, and had no part nor lot in the pious joys of his Presbyterian family, nor ever seemed to suffer from this deprivation." If Bence Blankenship's father was the village drunk, Sam's father was the village atheist. As was his wont, brother Orion, portrayed as Oscar Carpenter in the unfinished "Hellfire Hotchkiss" (written in 1897), a "creature of enthusiasms" with unsettled religious convictions, waffled like a spinning top among the Methodist Sunday school, then "the Campbellite Sunday school," then the Baptist and Presbyterian churches. As a character declares in *The American Claimant*, "I think he was a Mohammedan or something last week." Orion "belonged to as many as five different religious denominations," Sam asserted in 1879.[37]

Sam was more constant if less faithful. During his first year in Hannibal, he attended Sunday school at the Old Ship of Zion Methodist Church on the town square. His teacher was the local stonemason, Joshua Richmond, whom he came to admire. From the ages of five to seven, he recalled, "I was under Mr. Richmond's spiritual care every now and then." Under the tutelage of this "most kind and gentle-spirited man" Sam "became interested in Satan, and wanted to find out all I could about him"—or so he claimed. Hardly attracted to religious orthodoxy even as a child, he also concluded that the Prodigal Son was "the stupidest youth that ever lived, to go away from his father's palace where he had a dozen courses for dinner, and wore handsome clothes, and had fast horses, and dogs, and plenty of money to spend, and could go to the circus whenever he wanted to." Soon after his mother and sister Pamela joined the Presbyterian Church in February 1841, he began to attend services with them. As he testified in 1866, "I was brought up a Presbyterian"—he had been "sprinkled in infancy" and considered "that as conferring the rank of Brevet Presbyterian"—and he nominally identified as a Presbyterian for the rest of his life. He was attracted to the austere theology of the denomination: "The heaven and hell of the wildcat religions" such as spiritualism "are vague and ill defined but there is nothing mixed about the Presbyterian heaven and hell. The Presbyterian hell is all misery; the heaven all happiness." In any event, he learned from the Presbyterians, as W. D. Howells later noted, "to fear God and dread the Sunday School." Or as Dixon Wecter put it, Sam Clemens "did not believe in Hell, but he was afraid of it." His Presbyterian Sunday school teacher was David L. Garth, a slaveholder, grain merchant, owner of the local tobacco shop, and the father of his classmate and friend John Garth. In 1885, as he wrote his friend Charles Warren Stoddard, he looked back with "shuddering horror upon the days" in his adolescence "when I believed I believed." "To this day," he told Paine in old age, "I cherish an unappeasable bitterness against the unfaithful guardians of my young life, who not only permitted but compelled me to read an unexpurgated Bible through before I was 15 years old. None can do that and ever draw a clean, sweet breath again this side of the grave."[38]

Surprisingly, Sam harbored an ambition in adolescence to become a minister. It never occurred to him, he later joked, "that a preacher could be damned. It looked like a safe job." The "only genuine ambition I ever had," he wrote his nephew Sammy Moffett in 1866, was to preach the Gospel, "but somehow I never had any qualification for it *but* the ambition." He had admitted to Orion a year earlier that "he could not supply myself with the necessary stock in trade—*i.e.* religion" and that he "never had a 'call' in that direction, anyhow, & my aspirations were the very ecstasy of presumption." Still, he always counted liberal-minded ministers—those "fast nags of the cloth," he once called them—among his closest friends. As late as 1902, during his final trip to Hannibal, he candidly admitted that as a child he had "once started out to be" a clergyman and had wanted to stand in the Presbyterian pulpit "and give instructions—but I was never asked until today. My ambition of two generations ago has been satisfied at last."[39]

The religious sect that exerted the greatest influence on young Sam Clemens was perhaps the Disciples of Christ, or Campbellites, so named for their founders Thomas Campbell, a former Presbyterian, and his son Alexander. Harold K. Bush Jr. suggests that the group "was of great interest" to Sam because the "Campbellites were religious rebels." He "found aspects of the teachings of both Campbell and [his disciple Barton] Stone rather attractive, especially their willingness to question ossified belief and tradition," an element of the come-outer tradition of evangelicalism. Yet in advocating the restoration of "primitive Christianity," the Campbellites also appealed to baser instincts. The sect was virulently anti-Catholic, theological allies of the Know-Nothings of the 1840s and 1850s. The religious bias was deeply ingrained in Campbellite doctrine, which in its most extreme form identified the pope with the Antichrist, the "whore of Babylon" or the beast prophesied in the book of Revelation. Alexander Campbell belittled "the impious and arrogant pretensions of the haughty and tyrannical See of Rome," the "pretended vicar of Christ" on Earth, and equated Catholicism with such "antichristian" powers as Islam, paganism, and atheism. In the same vein, Orion once editorialized in the *Hannibal Journal* that the Catholic Church was a form of blight that threatened "to stretch over us her icy hand and bring upon us everlasting winter and barren desolation." Catholics were so unwelcome in Hannibal that the first Catholic church was not built there until 1854, the year after Sam left town.[40]

Sam's lifelong antipathy to Catholicism was stoked, ironically, by the Campbellite sermons he heard as a child, and he never completely outgrew the zeitgeist of anti-Catholic prejudice and superstition in which he was raised. He once admitted that he had been "educated to enmity toward everything that is Catholic, and sometimes, in consequence of this, I find it much easier to discover Catholic faults than Catholic merits."[41] He betrayed his anti-Catholic prejudice in February 1855 by reporting from St. Louis that a "new Catholic paper (bad luck to it)" was "soon to be established" there "for the purpose of keeping the Know Nothing organ straight." Hank Morgan eerily echoes the anti-Catholic bias of the Campbellites (and others) in chapter 8 of *A Connecticut Yankee in King Arthur's Court* (1889): "that awful power, the Roman Catholic Church" in only "two or three centuries" had "converted a nation of men to a nation of worms."[42] In context, then, the Battle of the Sand Belt that closes the novel is nothing less than Armageddon, the apocalyptic final war between the forces of holiness and evil—in this case, the Roman Church.

The Campbellites certainly left their mark on young Sam. Barton W. Stone, Campbell's chief lieutenant, was the grandfather of the Bowen brothers, Will, Sam, and Bart, the latter even named for him. In 1839, before she became a Presbyterian, Pamela Clemens was recruited to the sect by Stone's daughter Amanda, the Bowen boys' mother.[43] Even Marshall Clemens "inclined to the Campbellites" if to any church, according to Orion.[44] The original Campbellite congregation in Hannibal was established in March 1843, when Sam was only seven, and within a year it had grown to fifty members. They soon built a brick meetinghouse on Center Street. Other Campbellites with whom Sam was acquainted in his childhood were his classmate John Robards, whose father was an elder in the church; John's sister Sally Robards, who later married Bart Bowen; John Briggs's sister Artemisia, one of Sam's first sweethearts; and John D. Dawson, the model for Archibald Ferguson, the Scotch schoolmaster in "Schoolhouse Hill," and the prurient, sadistic schoolmaster Dobbins in *Tom Sawyer*.[45]

Sam Clemens also knew Barton Stone, who held a revival five miles southwest of Hannibal in mid-October 1844, soon after the measles epidemic began to wane; it may have been the revival mentioned in *Tom Sawyer*. In an autobiographical note probably written in the mid-1870s, he recalled a "Campbellite revival. All converted but me. All sinners again in a week," exactly as in the novel. The identification of the revival in the novel with the

Campbellites is even more explicit in the original manuscript. There Sam wrote, then deleted, this line: "As usual, the first revival had bred a second, the second a third, and so on, the Presbyterians following close upon the heels of the Methodists, & the Camp—." In a lecture in 1871, too, Sam reminisced about a prank he and Will Bowen ostensibly played on Barton Stone about this time. They "got hold of a pack of cards and indulged heavily in euchre." A minister was "stopping at the [Bowen] house, and to secrete the cards they placed them in his black gown, which hung in a closet." While the minister stood in the robe baptizing converts in the Mississippi a few days later, "the cards commenced to float upon the water, the first cards being a couple of bowers and three aces." One of the boys—probably Will—"got walloped" by his mother, though Sam later protested, "I don't see how [the minister] could help going out on a hand like that." The anecdote is probably apocryphal—Sam admitted in 1906 that he had "invented that story forty years ago." In any event, after leading another revival near Columbia, Missouri, in late October 1844, Barton Stone fell ill, returned on horseback to Hannibal, and died on November 9 in his daughter Amanda's home. After his death, Stone's widow moved from Illinois to the Bowen house, where she died thirteen years later.[46]

Alexander Campbell also preached in Hannibal while on a tour of northeastern Missouri in the fall of 1845. He spoke in Palmyra on November 3 and traveled the next day, he reported, "to Hannibal, an infant but rapidly rising mercantile city, on the bank of the Mississippi. While there we . . . enjoyed a visit to Mr. [Samuel] Bowen's, at whose residence departed this life the venerable Barton W. Stone. His daughter . . . is one of the most kind and amiable of human kind, and all worth of the admiration and affection of those who know the value and liveliness of female excellence." Campbell delivered a sermon in Hannibal on November 4 that inspired "a prodigious excitement," as Sam Clemens remembered sixty years later. "The farmers and their families drove or tramped into the village from miles around to get a sight of the illustrious Alexander Campbell and to have a chance to hear him preach." The church on Center Street was too small to seat all of them, however, and Sam recalls that he spoke "in the open air in the public square, and that was the first time in my life that I had realized what a mighty population this planet contains when you get them all together." Strangely enough, Tom Blankenship, the younger brother of Bence and the model for the character Huckleberry Finn, was dressed in hand-me-downs by the mothers of John Robards and Barney Farthing, the latter another of Sam's classmates, and sent to hear Campbell's sermon. As incongruous as it may seem, Tom Blankenship may have been temporarily "converted," much as Huck greets Tom after the revival "with a Scriptural quotation."[47]

Alexander Campbell returned to Hannibal in 1852 while on a fund-raising tour for Bethany College, a school he had founded in Virginia. He arrived on Sunday, November 14, some two weeks before Sam's seventeenth birthday. The village had "greatly improved and grown since my first visit in 1845," Campbell discovered. "It is now quite a commercial place." He delivered two talks, the first on Sunday in the sanctuary of the Campbellite church "on the Christian Religion, and one on Monday, on the great subject of Education, domestic and scholastic, with reference to the whole destiny of man, and especially in his moral and religious relations and obligations to the church and to the state." A short piece in the *Hannibal Journal*, almost certainly written by Orion, noted that Campbell had preached "to very large audiences. His sermon on Sunday was the most instructive and one of the best arguments we have ever heard from any pulpit." The poor but proud Campbellites in Hannibal pledged some five hundred dollars toward the Bethany College endowment before Campbell's departure. On his part, Sam remembered that when he "was seventeen years old and miserably ignorant, the great preacher, Alexander Campbell, came to our town and preached. . . . Nothing was talked of for days afterward" but his "wonderful sermon. . . . He was a very grim, frozen, unapproachable man, and very particular about every little thing."[48] Campbell's influence was felt throughout northeast Missouri for years to come, even after his death in 1866. The Paris Female Seminary in Monroe County and the Palmyra Female Seminary in Marion County were both founded by graduates of Bethany College.

Sam eventually realized the futility of religious fanaticisms. As early as 1860 he observed to Orion that "what a man wants with religion in these breadless times passes my comprehension." He might as well have referred to religious faith as the opiate of the people. In the first chapter of *Tom Sawyer Abroad* (1894) Huck remarks on an eclipse "that started a revival, same as it always does"—likely an allusion to the solar eclipse in Missouri that occurred on July 8, 1851, when Sam was fifteen. (He also ridiculed the superstitious souls who considered an eclipse a sign from God in chapter 6 of *A Connecticut Yankee in King Arthur's Court*.) In his essay "The New Wildcat Religion" (1866) he remembered when "Methodist camp-meetings and Campbellite revivals used to stock the asylums with religious lunatics." As late as 1888, in taking notes for an incident he planned to include in *A Connecticut Yankee*, Sam jotted in his journal that he "made a Campbellite out of the skunk man, for this would require him to bathe & keep clean."[49]

Sam recorded in his autobiography another vivid boyhood recollection of Alexander Campbell. Not surprisingly, it is demonstrably untrue. The anecdote is based on an entry jotted in his notebook, again probably in 1888:

> Rev. Alex Campbell, founder of the Campbellites, gently reproved our apprentice, Wales McCormick, <once,> on separate occasions, for saying Great God! When <"> Great Scott would have done as well, & for <us[in]> committing the Unforgiven Sin when *any* other form of express would have been a million times better. Weeks afterward, that inveterate light-head had his turn, & corrected the Reverend. In correcting the pamphlet-proof of one of Campbell's great sermons, Wales changed "Great God!" to "Great Scot," & changed Father, Son & Holy Ghost to Father, Son & Caesar's Ghost. In overrunning, he reduced it to Father, Son & Co., to keep from overrunning. And Jesus *H.* Christ.

As Sam recounted the events in 1906, Campbell had preached a sermon in Hannibal that his local followers wanted to have printed. But Wales McCormick, the apprentice printer, accidentally left out a few words, and to save type and time in correcting the mistake he reduced "Jesus Christ" to "J.C." Campbell was outraged, admonishing McCormick, "So long as you live, don't you ever diminish the Saviour's name again. Put it *all* in." To exact revenge, so the story goes, McCormick reset the final three pages of the sermon to "improve upon the great preacher's admonition. He enlarged the offending J.C. into Jesus H. Christ."[50]

All Clemens biographers who mention this episode—among them DeLancey Ferguson, Andrew Hoffman, Justin Kaplan, Ron Powers, and Dixon Wecter—accept this account at face value. Instead, it should be discounted at least as much as a Civil War greenback; it is another example of Sam's creative remembering. There are several reasons to doubt its veracity, especially the many discrepancies between the notebook and autobiographical versions of events. For example, in his notebook Clemens recalled that Campbell "gently reproved" the apprentice, whereas in his autobiography he remembered that Campbell delivered a "very stern" reprimand. More to the point, Sam did not work alongside Wales McCormick in Joseph P. Ament's print shop on the two occasions Campbell visited Hannibal. In November 1845, when he was only nine years old, he had not yet been apprenticed to Ament, and by November 1852 he had left Ament's employ to set type for his brother. Nor is there a bibliographical record of any sermon by Campbell ever published in Hannibal. Clemens likely (mis)remembered, instead, the circumstances surrounding the publication of a sermon by a local member of the Missouri Conference of the Methodist Episcopal Church, William G. Caples, in 1849—the only pamphlet known to have been set in type in

Hannibal during the period Sam was apprenticed to Ament. Titled *Justification, or the Pardon of Sin: Its Nature and the Means of Obtaining It*, its author argues an arcane theological point: that sprinkling is just as efficacious as (or no more or less efficacious than) immersion, or "water baptism."[51] Nor does Caples's printed sermon contain any reference to "Jesus H. Christ."

Marshall Clemens's personal (mis)fortunes reached their nadir in 1845–46. In the spring of 1845 he moved the office he occupied as justice of the peace to a local commission house, where he moonlighted as a clerk. "I did not succeed in making such arrangements as would enable me to go into business advantageously on my own acc[oun]t," he wrote his daughter Pamela on May 5, "and thought it best therefore not to attempt it at present." The family moved across Hill Street from the house where they had lived for over a decade to the second story of Grant's Drug Store, the same building where Sam Smarr had died a few weeks earlier. They paid no rent, but Jane Clemens cooked for Orville Grant's family. In late 1846, in revenge for the suit Marshall Clemens had filed against him a few years earlier, William Beebe obtained a $290 note Clemens owed and sued him in retaliation. The judge awarded Beebe both the amount of the note and $126.50 in damages, and on December 17 he was granted a writ of attachment ordering the sheriff to sell "the goods and chattels and real estate of the said John M. Clemens" to satisfy the judgment. The sheriff could find nothing of value to sell.[52]

By the spring of 1847, however, Marshall Clemens was finally poised to revive his legal career. He worked during the winter of 1846–47 to found a Masonic college in Hannibal. He became active in town meetings and chaired a committee that recommended the construction of what eventually became the Hannibal and St. Joseph Railroad. He served on a committee that tried to redraw the line between Marion and Ralls Counties, and he lobbied to extend the National Road (which ran from Cumberland, Maryland, to Springfield, Illinois) another hundred miles to Hannibal.[53] By early 1847 he was nominated by the Whigs for the office of clerk of the local circuit court and selected as a delegate to the Whig state party convention.[54]

Then calamity came. Returning on horseback from a campaign swing through Palmyra in a "storm of sleet and rain" in early March 1847, according to Sam, Marshall arrived in Hannibal "in a half-frozen condition," contracted pleurisy and pneumonia, and died on March 24 at the age of forty-eight. He may have suffered mercury poisoning as the result of self-medication that compromised his immune system and hastened his death. According to Sam, he experienced a deathbed conversion ten minutes before he took his last breath. Sam recorded two different versions of his last words in his *Autobiography*, neither of them very uplifting. In his dictation on January

13, 1906, he recalled that in the throes of his distress his father "put his arm around my sister's neck and drew her down and kissed her, saying 'Let me die'" without so much as bidding his wife or sons farewell. Elsewhere in his autobiography, however, Sam remembered that Marshall Clemens charged his entire family to "Cling to the land and wait; let nothing beguile it away from you." Yet a third version of his father's final words is offered in the novel *The Gilded Age*, where Silas Hawkins tells the family, "I am leaving you in cruel poverty. I have been—so foolish—so short-sighted. But courage! A better day is—is coming. Never lose sight of the Tennessee Land! Be wary. There is wealth stored up for you there—wealth that is boundless!" In any case, Marshall's death certainly left the family in cruel poverty. "We were about to be comfortable once more, after several years of grinding poverty and privation," Sam observed in his dictation, but "our splendid new fortune was snatched from us and we were in the depths of poverty again." Marshall Clemens was buried a few days later in the Old Baptist Cemetery atop Holliday's Hill—the same cemetery where Huck and Tom witness Dr. Robinson's murder by the moral monster Injun Joe in chapter 9 of *Tom Sawyer*. So traumatic was his father's death that Sam wrote his daughter Clara on its anniversary in 1910: "My father died this day 63 years ago. I remember all about it quite clearly."[55]

Still worse, he viewed the autopsy. In a notebook entry dated October 10, 1903, Sam noted that in 1847 he had observed the "post mortem of my uncle through keyhole." Of course, it is a disguised reference to Marshall Clemens. Sam had no uncle who died in 1847. That is, he apparently watched the operation performed on his father's body by the family physician, Dr. Hugh Meredith. Such a medical procedure was unusual in 1847 except in cases in which the cause of death was unknown. What did the autopsy reveal? A clue appears in a letter Howells sent Clemens in 1880 after reading a draft of Orion's autobiography: "Don't let any one else see those passages about the autopsy. The light on your father's character is most pathetic." The inference is inescapable: the autopsy revealed that Marshall Clemens had contracted a venereal disease. As Orion also noted, during the last years of his father's hard-knock life "he bought Cooke's pills by the box and took one or more daily."[56] Cooke's pills and blue mass pills, both of which were laced with an active ingredient of mercury chloride, or calomel, were readily available for as little as a dollar a pound over the counter at any drugstore in Hannibal and were standard allopathic treatments for conditions such as tuberculosis, toothache, constipation, and syphilis. Marshall Clemens may have suffered from a venereal disease for years. If so, his wife had not contracted it, suggesting that they had long since stopped having marital relations.

CHAPTER 3

Hannibal

I can picture that old time to myself now . . . : the white town drowsing
in the sunshine of a summer's morning.

—"Old Times on the Mississippi"

"Orion came to the rescue," Samuel Clemens conceded in 1906. After
Marshall Clemens's death, his eldest son at the tender age of twenty-one
became the breadwinner and titular head of the family. After the funeral
Orion returned to St. Louis, where he was setting type for the *St. Louis Reveille*, and from his weekly wage of ten dollars he mailed three dollars home to
Hannibal. Pamela, who played piano and guitar, moved forty miles to Paris,
Missouri, to teach music. "I have never found any difficulty as yet in getting
scholars," she gloated. The rest of the family continued to live on the second
floor of Grant's Drug Store. "Thus we got along," according to Sam, "but it
was pretty hard sledding."[1]

Orion had never aspired to a career as printer or newspaper editor. "I embarked in the business with no more partiality for it than for any other occupation," he remembered. Instead, he craved a career in politics. "If I could
have been so employed that daily practice in the art of speaking would have
been part of my duty, my life would have been full of bliss during all my
working hours," but "that had been forbidden by my father." He added, with
no little resentment,

> His pleasure in knowing that I was so engaged must have been slight, com-
> pared with the happiness I might have enjoyed if I had been permitted to pur-
> sue a course warmed by the fervor and illumined by the light of my childish
> dreams. . . . There being no pleasure in the mechanical part of the business,
> and no hope of attaining a position where I could work at editing, free from
> the embarrassments of business, I began to yearn for a chance to get away
> from the office, and rest and breathe fresh air.

Orion returned to Hannibal on weekends: he taught a Sunday school class
there and delivered an Independence Day speech in the village on Sunday,
July 4. The family also received an unexpected windfall soon after Marshall

Clemens's death: $150 for the sale of eight hundred acres of the Tennessee land.[2] Orion earned a little extra cash as the Hannibal correspondent for the *Reveille*, owned and edited by Joe Field, a humorist and the father of Kate Field, a lecturer and journalist with whom Sam Clemens would often cross paths in the future. Orion was probably paid a dollar or two for each of his columns, all signed Lorio, nearly an anagram of Orion.

These columns fill in some blanks in the history of Hannibal. In his auto-biography, Sam reminisces about the "first negro-minstrel show I ever saw. It must have been in the early '40s. In our village of Hannibal we had not heard of it . . . before, and it burst upon us as a glad and stunning surprise. The show remained a week, and gave a performance every night." The format of this entertainment was carefully structured, if not entirely scripted, with standard makeup and costumes and assigned roles for the end men or comic stooges and the caricatured middleman or interlocutor. To be sure, the hu-morous songs and broad dialect exploited the stereotype of the "comic dark-ie" almost always played by white men in blackface (which was created by the application of burned cork), though the most popular shows also expressed topical social satire. As Eric Lott has explained, "acting black" encompassed "a whole social world of irony, negotiation, violence, and learning." Accord-ing to Albert Bigelow Paine, after the first minstrel show to visit Hannibal pulled up stakes and left, Sam "yearned for a brief period to be a magnificent 'middle man' or even the 'end-man' of that combination." Sam wrote in *The Adventures of Tom Sawyer* (1876) that the "first of all the Negro minstrel shows" to come to St. Petersburg, the fictionalized Hannibal, "made a sen-sation," and in "Old Times on the Mississippi" (1875) he added that "the first negro minstrel show that came to our section left us all suffering to try that kind of life." That show was almost certainly the one mentioned by Lorio in his Hannibal dispatch to the *Reveille* dated April 27, 1847, where he reported that the "small boys of our city were thrown into a high state of excitement this morning by the sudden appearance among us of the 'Sable Brothers,' and the subsequent pasting up, on all the corners, of big hand-bills, with big type in them, announcing that they (the 'Brothers') would do certain wonderful things at a certain place mentioned, and beginning at a certain hour."[3] The Sable Brothers, featuring the minstrel pioneer William S. Cleveland, also performed in New York City in 1847. They are the only minstrel troupe Sam is known to have seen in boyhood.

Another Lorio letter establishes the date that the first "mesmerizer" or hypnotist visited the village. In his autobiography Sam reminisced about this "exciting" appearance. He thought the year was 1850. "As to that I am not sure," he allowed, "but I know the month—it was May." The mesmer-izer's visit in fact occurred in May 1847. As Lorio reported to the *Reveille* on May 20, "two gentlemen" arrived in Hannibal "a few days ago," one to lecture on mesmerism and the other to practice it on townspeople selected from the audience. The *Hannibal Gazette* printed a few additional details about the performers, a duo named Sparhawk and Layton: their "remarks and experiments" were "highly interesting," and their "subject (who resides in the city) seemed fully under the magnetic influence" and "anyone who doubted was desired to examine him." They performed every night for two weeks in Hawkins' Saloon and charged only ten cents' admission.[4] Sam was only eleven at the time.

His age is significant because of the role he played in the mesmerist's performances. As he explained in his autobiography, "The village had heard of mesmerism in a general way, but had not encountered it yet." Sam believed that he had been at the time "fourteen or fifteen years old—the age at which a boy is willing to endure all things, suffer all things, short of death by fire." By the fourth evening of the performances, he "had a burning desire to be a subject myself" and to replace his rival, a journeyman printer, onstage. Selected from the audience, as he tells the story, he gazed at a spinning disk until he "began to nod" and pretended to be in a trance. At the command of the hypnotist, he "fled from snakes, passed buckets at a fire," and "made love to imaginary girls and kissed them. . . . I was cautious at first, and watchful, being afraid the professor would discover that I was an impostor," but soon he simply acted out of impulse, and the mesmerist went along with the ruse, claiming he was ordering the child around telepathically. "After that fourth night, that proud night, that triumphant night, I was the only subject," he recalled, and "I performed alone, every night, the rest of the fortnight. . . . When the magician's engagement closed there was but one person in the village who did not believe in mesmerism, and I was the one." He was to remain thereafter "an implacable and unpersuadable disbeliever in mesmerism and hypnotism for close upon fifty years." In both *Tom Sawyer* and *Adventures of Huckleberry Finn* (1885), mesmerists are nothing more than frauds. In *Tom Sawyer*, a "phrenologist and a mesmerizer" comes to St. Petersburg to dupe the townspeople for a week or two, and in *Huck Finn* the Duke brags that he sometimes takes "a turn to mesmerism and phrenology when there's a chance." According to his working notes for the novel, in fact, Sam considered adding a scene featuring "the mesmeric foolishness, with Huck & the king for performers." Ironically, when Sam confessed to his mother during a visit to Hannibal thirty-five years later that he had been a willing stooge, merely pretending to be in a trance, she refused to believe "that I had invented my visions myself; she said it was folly: that I was only a child at the time and could not have done it."[5] Even Orion thought Sam was lying.

Minstrels and mesmerists were not the only entertainers to visit the village. Conveniently located on the Mississippi River and with a growing population, Hannibal became a popular stop on the circus circuit. According to Donald H. Welsh, "Circuses were common in Hannibal, three appearing in 1847 alone," including Mabie's Circus, Rockwell & Company's Mammoth Circus, and Turner's Menagerie & Circus. The popular circus clown Dan Rice performed in the village in 1848. On the Fourth of July in 1849, Raymond's Menagerie appeared in Hannibal, and the next year Stokes' Mammoth Circus played the village twice. It's little wonder that in *Tom Sawyer* the boys play circus "in tents made of rag carpeting" and that Huck tells Tom that with his share of the buried treasure they expect to discover he will "go to every circus that comes along." Sam remembered in "Old Times on the Mississippi," too, that whenever a circus came to Hannibal "it left us all burning to become clowns." In chapter 22 of *Huck Finn*, the eponymous hero actually attends a circus in Bricksville, another incarnation of Hannibal; and in the fragment "Hellfire Hotchkiss" (written in 1897) the title character is "on hand . . . with many others, at sunrise" to "see the elephant free of charge" when the circus promenades through town on its way south for the winter.[6]

If Orion's religious convictions were unsettled, his political principles were unwavering: pro-Union and antislavery. Like Abraham Lincoln he opposed slavery, but he was never a radical abolitionist. Instead, he was a meliorist who favored gradual emancipation. Like Lincoln, he became an ardent Republican when the Whig Party dissolved. He supported the Fugitive Slave Act that (temporarily) preserved the Union. In short, only a sliver of what Sam once said of him in the character of Oliver Hotchkiss in "Schoolhouse Hill" (1897–1908) is true: "He changed his principles with the moon, his politics with the weather, and his religion with his shirt." He "missed his vocation—he should have been a weather-vane." On the contrary, according to Minnie Brashear, Orion was "the greatest single influence" on Sam during his adolescence, becoming Sam's surrogate father after the death of Marshall Clemens. "He was always truthful; he was always sincere; he was always honest and honorable," Sam said of Orion in his autobiography.[7]

Orion has been unfairly caricatured by Twain scholars over the years as a callow will-o'-the wisp, mostly as a result of his brother's sibling rivalry. Sam referred derisively, for example, to "the pathetic realities of Orion's life" in his "Autobiography of a Damned Fool" (written in 1877). He wrote W. D. Howells in 1879 that Orion was "a field which grows richer and richer the more he mulches it with each new topdressing of religion or other guano" and that his older brother "had mental perception but no mental proportion." Following Sam's lead, James O'Donnell Bennett called Orion "the Village Idiot," and Seymour Gross described him as "one of the strangest fellows ever born." Dixon Wecter seems to have missed the irony of his own statement that "Orion, Sam's ne'er-do-well senior by ten years," was appointed by President Lincoln in 1861 as the "Secretary of the Territory of Nevada." Yet Fred W. Lorch fairly concludes that "it would be unsafe to rely upon Sam's estimate of Orion."[8] It is true enough that Orion's life pales in comparison to his younger brother's, but he was hardly the bumbler of legend. In fact, he was more progressive on racial issues than was Sam, and he was uncommonly successful until the age of thirty-eight, when he suffered the devastating loss of his only child.

If we can trust Sam's autobiography or his faux autobiography of his brother, Orion read a life of Ben Franklin at the age of twelve and "at once set about making a Franklin of himself." The claim seems reasonable enough. According to the historian Louis B. Wright, "by a credible though partial perception" of Franklin's ideas, the Found(l)ing Father became the "high priest of the religion of commercial success." In "Villagers of 1840–3" (1897), the character Oscar Carpenter, modeled on Orion, writes his mother that he is "studying the life of Franklin and closely imitating him" by dividing his day "on the Franklin plan—eight hours for labor, eight for sleep, eight for study, meditation and exercise." Whatever the reason, Orion's stock began to rise when he was in his early twenties. He was elected president of the St. Louis Apprentices' Association and in that office met Edward Bates, a Whig politician and former slaveholder who in 1861 became Lincoln's attorney general and the first cabinet member in U.S. history to hail from west of the Mississippi. Orion delivered a temperance speech in Hannibal in 1848, sent Bates a copy of it, and solicited career advice. Bates replied on March 8 "that no man could become a good editor of a newspaper or a statesman without being well acquainted with the civil and political history of his Country, including Constitutional law." Orion closely followed Bates's career, if not his advice, and editorially endorsed him for vice president on the Whig ticket in 1852. In a profile of Orion syndicated in newspapers across the country in 1892, he was said to rival his brother Sam "in conversational powers, and at almost every turn, upon almost any subject, there is a gleam of humor that fastens his thought to his hearer's mind." Even Sam sometimes admitted that Orion was a genius in his own idiosyncratic fashion: with "a grave mien and big earnest eyes," he had "a precocious intellect, and a voracious appetite for books and study. He had no playmates, of course; he had nothing to offer them, they had nothing to offer him."[9]

No doubt Orion was absentminded and easily distracted. His mother remembered that he "always was the most forgetful boy. . . . If I sent him for a pail of water he was just as likely to come back and tell me he couldn't find any as he was to bring me a pail of chips instead of water." Some of the stories told about him by Sam's biographers—none of them verifiable now—make him out to be an utter buffoon: accidentally stumbling into bed with two maiden ladies, calling on a sweetheart in the middle of the night, leaving the church without his new wife after their wedding, drinking a glass of ink he mistook for fruit juice. But Orion's absentmindedness may have a simple explanation: he may have been born with attention deficit hyperactivity disorder (ADHD), a medical condition often associated with high intelligence, somnambulism, and night terrors or, as his brother might have said, the "fan-tods."

Sam exhibited the same classic symptoms as his brother. "I scatter from one interest to another, lingering nowhere," he once allowed. "I am not a bee, I am a lightning bug." Or, as he admitted in his autobiography, "I was born excited," and "if I saw a vision I emptied the dictionary onto it and lost the remnant of my mind into the bargain." As is common for children with ADHD, many of Sam's early friends were younger than he was: Will Bowen by a half year, John Briggs by a year and a half, and John Robards by four years.[10] His Virginia City friend and roommate Dan De Quille remembered that Sam

> was nervously overstrung and always in danger of a neurotic upset or explosion. . . . [E]vidently there was some neural derangement from the time of his birth. Things that wouldn't disquiet the average man would grate on him and set him wild, while just an ordinary annoyance hit with the force of an overpowering shock. . . . Even under the most favorable conditions he could never sleep well of nights. He would lie and read, or walk the room, or prowl all over the house during most of the hours he should have been sleeping; and you had to lock your door if you didn't wish to keep vigil with him.

Louis J. Budd has concluded, fairly enough, that Sam was "often hyperactive in private."[11]

Sam's boredom with rote learning was another telltale sign of the condition. He had graduated from Elizabeth Horr's dame school to Mary Ann Newcomb's Select School in the basement of the Presbyterian church, where his teachers were a Miss Torrey and later Miss Newcomb, who boarded with the Clemens family. Newcomb wore her hair in "ringlets" or "spit curls" and sported "a long sharp nose, and thin, colorless lips, and you could not tell her breast from her back if she had her head up a stovepipe hole looking for something in the attic," Sam recalled. She was also "a most disagreeable woman." He described her more succinctly in "Villagers of 1840–3" as an "old maid and thin." He reimagined her years later in the characters of Miss Watson in *Huck Finn*, the "tolerable slim old maid" who is the Widow

Douglas's sister, as well as Miss Pomeroy in "Schoolhouse Hill"; the "long and lean and flat-chested" Frau Stein in "No. 44, the Mysterious Stranger" (1902–8); and Mrs. Bangs in the unfinished "Autobiography of a Damned Fool." The first time that Huck mentions Miss Watson, in fact, she is schoolmarmish: she "took a set at me now with a spelling-book. She worked me middling hard for about an hour." She also admonishes Huck "to pray every day, and whatever I asked for I would get it. But it warn't so." Similarly, Sam learned to doubt the efficacy of prayer, or so he insisted in his autobiography, after Miss Newcomb told him that "whosoever prayed for a thing in earnestness and strong desire need not doubt that his prayer would be answered." He "did as much praying, during the next two or three days, as anyone in that town . . . but nothing came of it."[12]

At the age of nine or so Sam enrolled in the academy on Holliday's Hill kept by Samuel Cross, one of the cofounders, with Marshall Clemens, of the Hannibal Library Institute in 1843 and an elder at the Presbyterian church. Among his two dozen classmates were George Robards and Laura Hawkins. A "slender, pale, studious" boy, Robards was the only Latin pupil and, as a result, depending on Sam's mood when he was reminiscing, he was either "the envy and admiration of all the school" or an insufferable prig. Laura Hawkins Frazer recalled three quarters of a century later that she "must have liked Sam Clemens the very first time I saw him" because he "was different from the other boys. I didn't know then, of course, what it was that made him different, but afterward, when my knowledge of the world and its people grew, I realized that it was his natural refinement." She remembered the "fuzzy light curls all over his head that really ought to have belonged to a girl," much as Sam attributed to Tom Sawyer "short curls" that he considered "effeminate" and as he recalled in his autobiography his own "dense ruck of short curls."[13]

Over fifty years later, after receiving an honorary degree from the University of Missouri, Sam credited Cross in part with preparing him for the distinction. Newcomb's granddaughters claimed in 1935 that when Sam visited Hannibal in 1902 he had acknowledged his debt to their ancestor because "she compelled [him] to learn to read." That Sam paid Newcomb this compliment is highly unlikely, however. When he passed through the village in 1902 he had insisted instead that he had received "all the learning" required to fit him for the LLD from "Mrs. Horr, Miss Torrey, Mr. Dawson and Mr. Cross," pointedly omitting Newcomb. Elsewhere, however, he disparaged Cross's form of instruction, which emphasized memorization and recitation, and he defined school in *The Gilded Age* (1873) as "a place where tender young humanity devoted itself for eight or ten hours a day to learning incomprehensible rubbish by heart out of books and reciting it by rote, like parrots."

At Cross's school, he noted, "we had exhibitions once or twice a year," and he often ridiculed the popularity on these occasions of such banal declamation pieces as Felicia Hemans's poem "Casabianca" (aka "The Boy Stood on the Burning Deck"), a ballad about a heroic lad who remains at the helm of a fiery ship in a vain attempt to save his father's life. These programs failed to feature "a single line of original thought or expression." Instead, if a student "showed any original thought the people suspected that something was the matter with him."[14] Sam dramatized the tedium of the exhibitions in chapter 21 of *Tom Sawyer*, in which students declaim such ripe old chestnuts as Patrick Henry's "Give Me Liberty or Give Me Death" speech, Mary Ann Harris Gay's "A Missouri Maiden's Farewell to Alabama," and "The Boy Stood on the Burning Deck."

In short, Sam loathed the monotony of the classroom. As the protagonist declares in the unfinished "Boy's Manuscript" (ca. 1868), "I hate school. . . . It is *so* dull," and Tom Sawyer barely tolerates school, with its "captivity and fetters." Laura Hawkins remembered that Sam often "played hooky from school" and "cared nothing at all" for his assignments, and he recalled an occasion when Cross "thrashed" him for his misbehavior. John A. Fry, another of his classmates, recollected that Sam was "shiftless, lazy, and dadblasted tired—born tired. No study in him." In 1885, in the only interview Jane Clemens is known to have granted, she reminisced with a reporter for the *Chicago Inter-Ocean* about her famous son's resistance to the rigors of formal education. "Sam was always a good-hearted boy," she acknowledged, "but he was a very wild and mischievous one, and do what we would we could never make him go to school. This used to trouble his father and me dreadfully, and we were convinced that he would never amount to as much in the world as his brothers, because he was not nearly so steady and sober-minded as they were." Sometimes Sam's father would start him in the direction of Cross's school, she remembered,

> and in a little while would follow him to ascertain his whereabouts. There was a large stump on the way to the schoolhouse, and Sam would take his position behind that and as his father went past would gradually circle around it in such a way as to keep out of sight. Finally his father and the teacher both said it was of no use to try to teach Sam anything, because he was determined not to learn. But I never gave up. He was always a great boy for history and could never get tired of that kind of reading, but he hadn't any use for schoolhouses and textbooks.

When Marshall Clemens died, according to his widow, she thought then, if ever, was the proper time to make a lasting impression on the boy and work a change in him, so I took him by the hand and went with him into the room where the coffin was and in which the father lay, and with it between Sam and me I said to him that here in this presence I had some serious requests to make of him, and that I knew his word once given was never broken. . . . He turned his streaming eyes upon me and cried out, "Oh, mother, I will do anything, anything you ask of me except to go to school; I can't do that!"

It was, of course, "the very request I was going to make. Well, we afterward had a sober talk," and they compromised.[15] If Sam would continue to attend school, he could also work part-time for the *Hannibal Gazette*, the first Democratic paper in the village, founded in November 1846 and owned and edited by Henry La Cossitt. Sam was an apprentice and journeyman printer for the next nine years. He also worked at a variety of odd jobs: delivery boy, drugstore and grocery clerk, law student, apprentice in a blacksmith shop, and bookstore assistant. Had there "been a few more occupations to experiment on," he later mused, "I might have made a dazzling success at last." From the day his father died "until the end of 1856 or the first days of 1857," he added, "I worked—not diligently, not willingly, but fretfully, lazily, repiningly, complainingly, disgustedly, and always shirking the work when I was not watched."[16]

In lieu of (or in addition to) his formal schooling—"if playing hookey & getting licked for it may be called by that name," he joked—Sam was an autodidact and chimney-corner child, a book lover since childhood. "He got the hang of books in his cradle," Henry Watterson remembered. As an adolescent he was fond of Lord Byron's verse, George William Curtis's *Potiphar Papers*, Thomas Chandler Haliburton's comic *Clockmaker* stories featuring the Yankee wiseacre Sam Slick, and Frederick Marryat's sea novels. He was familiar with the works of the literary comedians George Horatio Derby (aka John Phoenix); Donald Grant Mitchell (aka Ik Marvel); B. P. Shillaber (aka Mrs. Partington); William Tappan Thompson, author of Major Jones's *Sketches of Travel* (1847); and Frances Miriam Whitcher (aka the Widow Bedott). The dime novelist Edward Z. C. Hudson (aka Ned Buntline) gave a lecture in Hannibal in November 1851, "Cuba and Her Martyrs," and a quarter of a century later Sam modeled some of Tom Sawyer's adventures on Buntline's sensational pirate tale *The Black Avenger of the Spanish Main* (1847).[17]

But Sam eventually outgrew his love for a couple of other canonical authors favored by juvenile readers. Like other adolescents, especially in the South, he enjoyed the Waverley novels of Sir Walter Scott, though forty years later in *Life on the Mississippi* (1883) he referred derisively to the "Walter Scott

Middle-Age sham civilization" and the "Sir Walter disease" that infected the chivalric ethos of the South, semiseriously blaming Scott for causing the Civil War: "Sir Walter had so large a hand in making" antebellum Southern character, he averred, "that he is in great measure responsible for the war." Sam expressed his disdain for the Waverley novels again in chapter 12 of *Huck Finn*, where three thieves trapped aboard a sinking steamboat named the *Walter Scott* represent the debased condition of the Old South prior to the war. In 1895 he tactfully told an interviewer that "Scott used a great many words where in our day we would get along with one or two," and as late as 1902 he claimed that he "could not read" Scott's novels "even as a child. . . . Their long descriptions, their false Wardour Street of antiquity, repelled me." Similarly, James Fenimore Cooper's Leatherstocking Tales were so popular among the boys in Hannibal that, Sam said, any of them "would have been proud of a 'strain' of Indian blood."[18] He eventually changed his mind about Cooper, too.

In mid-April 1847, three weeks after Marshall Clemens's death, John D. Dawson, a native Scot and devout Campbellite, opened still another private school in Hannibal. Sam enrolled, probably in the fall of 1847, and remained at least a year; the 1850 census indicated he had attended school within the previous twelve months. It was the last school he attended, and it was the one that most resembles Dobbins's school in *Tom Sawyer*. "If I wanted to describe [Dawson's school] I could save myself the trouble by conveying the description of it to these pages from *Tom Sawyer*," Sam remarked in his autobiography. Among his classmates were Sally Robards; Nannie Owsley, the seven-year-old daughter of Sam Smarr's killer; and the schoolmaster's son Theodore, the original for the Model Boy, Willie Mufferson, the darling of all the mothers in *Tom Sawyer*. Theodore Dawson was "inordinately good, extravagantly good, offensively good, detestably good—and he had pop-eyes," Sam remembered, "and I would have drowned him if I had had a chance." As he described him elsewhere, the "Model Boy of my time—we never had but the one—was perfect: perfect in manners, perfect in dress, perfect in conduct, perfect in filial piety, perfect in exterior godliness; but at bottom he was a prig; and as for the contents of his skull, they could have changed place with the contents of a pie and nobody would have been the worse off for it but the pie." In one crucial way, however, art did not imitate life: Tom Sawyer finished the school year at Dobbins's school and began his summer vacation; Sam finished his year at Dawson's school and became a full-time apprentice in a print shop. A quarter century later, in *Roughing It* (1872), he claimed that he "had gone out into the world to shift for myself at the age of thirteen."[19] Not exactly. He may have gone to work at thirteen, but his mother lived nearby and her pantry door was always open.

In May 1848 Joseph P. Ament, the twenty-four-year-old owner of the *Missouri Courier*, moved the four-page weekly from Palmyra to Hannibal, bought the *Hannibal Gazette*, and merged the two papers. The next month, even as he completed his final year of formal education, Sam was apprenticed to Ament. As Jane Clemens explained, in a stunning understatement, "I concluded to let him go into a printing office to learn the trade, as I couldn't have him running wild. He did so, and has gradually picked up enough education to enable him to do about as well as those who were more studious in early life."[20] Much as Marshall Clemens apprenticed Orion in 1841 to reduce household expenses when his store and hotel in Hannibal failed, Jane apprenticed Sam to reduce household expenses after his father died.

The tasks performed by a printer's devil were menial and tedious, to say the least, and Sam was little more than an indentured servant. He not only collected money from subscribers by walking door-to-door but learned to sort and set 154 different pieces of type. He built Ament's fire on winter mornings, and

> I brought his water from the village pump; I swept out his office; I picked up his type from under his stand; and, if he was there to see, I put the good type in his case and the broken ones among the "hell matter"; and if he wasn't there to see, I dumped it all with the "pi" on the imposing stone. . . . I wetted down the paper Saturdays, I turned it Sundays—for this was a country weekly; I rolled, I washed the rollers, I washed the forms, I folded the papers, I carried them around at dawn Thursday mornings. . . . I enveloped the papers that were for the mail—we had a hundred town subscribers and three hundred and fifty county ones; the town subscribers paid in groceries and the country ones in cabbages and cordwood—when they paid at all, which was merely sometimes, and then we always stated the fact in the paper and gave them a puff; and if we forgot it they stopped the paper. Every man on the town list helped edit the thing; that is, he gave orders as to how it was to be edited; dictated its opinions, marked out its course for it, and every time the boss failed to connect, he stopped his paper.

Sam also claimed sixty years later that he "helped to edit the paper when no one was watching."[21]

He received no wages—merely room, board, and two suits of clothes a year, usually oversized hand-me-downs from Ament. Sam was only about half Ament's size, however, and when he wore one of his boss's old shirts "I felt as if I had on a circus tent. I had to turn the trousers up to my ears to make them short enough." Ament's apprentices, slaves, cook, and the cook's daughter "got but little variety in the way of food" at the table in the kitchen, Sam recalled, "and there wasn't enough of it anyway." He was sometimes so hungry that he stole potatoes and onions from Ament's root cellar and roasted them in the printing office. Two years after leaving Ament's employ, Sam scorned his former boss as a "diminutive chunk of human meat," a "*father of* NOTHING," and a "soft-soaper of Democratic rascality." Still, he made a couple of close

Figure 3. A daguerreotype of Samuel Clemens at age fifteen, 1850. Collection of Gary Scharnhorst.

friends in Ament's shop. His fellow apprentice Wales McCormick was "a reckless, hilarious, admirable creature; he had no principles, and was delightful company." McCormick was also the model for the irreverent "wandering comp" Doangivadam in "No. 44, the Mysterious Stranger": "He was a beauty, trim and graceful as Satan, and was a born masher and knew it." Writing to Sam over twenty years later, the jour printer Pet McMurry, his other friend in Ament's shop, remembered him as "a little sandy-headed, curly-headed boy . . . mounted upon a little box at the case, pulling away at a huge Cigar, or a diminutive pipe."[22] In the earliest photograph of Sam, a daguerreotype probably taken at Ballard's Dagnerrean Rooms on November 29, 1850, the day before his fifteenth birthday, he stands with his typecase in hand.

Sam picked up his lifelong tobacco habit as early as the age of eight, certainly before Marshall Clemens died. In 1882 he confessed that he "began to smoke immoderately when I was eight years old; that is, I began with one hundred cigars a month," and in 1906 he corroborated the fact: he had been "a smoker from my ninth year—a private one during the first two years, but a public one after that—that is to say, after my father's death." But he quit smoking for several months in the summer of 1850 when he joined the Cadets of Temperance. An affiliate of the Sons of Temperance, the Cadets promoted abstinence from liquor and tobacco. Sam was attracted less by the pledge of its members, as he admitted later, "not to smoke, never to drink or gamble, to keep the Sabbath, and not to steal watermelons" than by the regalia they wore during holiday parades, particularly their red merino sashes. "I was clothed like a conflagration," he wrote in "Autobiography of a Damned Fool." "I have never enjoyed any dress so much as I enjoyed that 'regalia.'" Elsewhere he allowed that "it was a pretty good sort of organization, and some of the very best boys in the village" belonged to it, including his brother Henry, John Briggs (the model for Ben Rogers in *Tom Sawyer*), Jimmy McDaniel (who, ironically, eventually became a cigarmaker), John Meredith, and Tom Nash. Sam joined the Cadets, he conceded, even though the by-laws of the organization "didn't allow a boy to smoke, or drink or swear, but I thought I never could be truly happy till I wore one of those stunning red scarfs and walked in procession when a distinguished citizen died." In *Tom Sawyer*, Sam re-created his predicament:

> Tom joined the new order of Cadets of Temperance, being attracted by the showy character of their "regalia." He promised to abstain from smoking, chewing, and profanity as long as he remained a member. Now he found out a new thing—namely, that to promise not to do a thing is the surest way in the world to make a body want to go and do that very thing. Tom soon found himself tormented with a desire to drink and swear.

He tolerated the prohibitions for four months, but in the end "there were not enough holidays to support" his membership in the group. He marched in his regalia on May Day and the Fourth of July 1850 but, as he later said, "you can't keep a juvenile moral institution alive on two displays of its sash per year," and "never an infernal distinguished citizen died during the whole time" he belonged to it.[23] After the second parade, he quit.

The leading industry of Hannibal was meatpacking—particularly pork. If Chicago was the "hog butcher of the world," then Hannibal was the hog butcher of the region—what Carl Sandburg might have called the city of the pig shoulders. Dixon Wecter described the village as a "miniature porkopolis." The three packing companies in the town, with their pigsties on Bear Creek, a half mile from the Clemens house, employed three hundred workers in season. With a forty-thousand-square-foot slaughterhouse, the firm of Samuel & Moss was among the largest pork and beef packinghouses in the United States. According to Lorio in one of his Hannibal letters to the *St. Louis Reveille*, the senior partner, William Samuel, "cleared some twenty thousand dollars by dealing in pork" during the fall and winter of 1846–47. The junior partner, Russell Moss, was the father of Mary Moss, one of Sam's classmates, whom he thought "very sweet and pretty at 16 or 17." Two new slaughterhouses were built on Bear Creek in 1846, and Dowling & Company, one of the rivals of Samuel & Moss, built a twenty-thousand-square-foot slaughterhouse a year later that enabled the business to ship five hundred barrels of processed meat and lard per day. The packers paid local farmers a premium price, about five cents per pound for porkers that weighed at least 180 pounds, and the *Missouri Courier* reported in December 1849 that together the "slaughtering houses kill from 1000 to 1500 [hogs] per day" during the late fall and winter.[24]

The result was environmental disaster. The farmers herded their droves through the streets of Hannibal en route to slaughter, and not until 1911 were the streets cleaned routinely. The first town council considered the packinghouses a public health hazard and decreed "that no vegetable matter, unclean substance or filthy water be thrown into the streets or into Bear Creek, that refuse from the slaughterhouses be conducted into the Mississippi and out into the current so that it could not return to the shore."[25] But the ordinance did not prevent tons of offal from draining into the river. Bear Creek became so polluted with dissolved fat it was nicknamed Soap Alley. For obvious reasons, the preachers baptized their converts and boys went swimming in the creek upstream from the packing plants or in the Mississippi above the mouth of the creek.

All of this may begin to explain the ubiquity of swine in Sam's writing. "Historical Exhibition—A No. 1 Ruse" (1852), a comic monologue and one of the earliest pieces that can be confidently attributed to him, tells of "a show of some kind" with the "attractive title" of "Napoleon Crossing the Rhine" on display at a local store. The exhibit turns out to be a pork bone (a bony part, or Bonaparte) crossing a pig rind (the Rhine)—an example of the coarse, lowbrow humor of the tavern and docks. In *Tom Sawyer* the children play with pig bladders from the slaughterhouses, and Sam also mentioned hogs rooting contentedly in the unpaved streets of towns in *The Gilded Age*, *Huck Finn*, *A Connecticut Yankee in King Arthur's Court* (1889), *Life on the Mississippi*, and the "Tupperville-Dobbsville" fragment (ca. 1876–80). In *Life on the Mississippi*, Sam also mentioned Bear Creek as the open sewer and "famous breeder of chills and fever in its day." The prevailing breezes down the river valley usually wafted the stench from the stockyards south, away from the center of town, but sometimes it hung in the air like a miasma. The richest person in town, Melicent Holliday, the model for the "fair, smart," and "good-hearted" Widow Douglas in *Tom Sawyer* and *Huck Finn*, lived in a mansion at the crest of the highest hill in the region, upwind from the packinghouses, to escape the stench below. As Huck declares in "Tom Sawyer's Conspiracy" (1897–1902), the "polecats couldn't stand" the stink of the slaughterhouses, "where the creek comes in. . . . [I]t smelt like the very [dam]nation." Then there were the tanyards in the ravine where various incarnations of "the fragrant town drunkard" Jimmy Finn (Pap Finn in *Huck Finn* and Si Higgins in "Autobiography of a Damned Fool") sleep with the hogs and die in a tanning vat "of a combination of delirium tremens and spontaneous combustion." According to Sam's autobiographical dictation, Judge Clemens once tried to reform Jimmy Finn "but did not succeed," much like the "new judge" in St. Petersburg who fails to reform Pap in chapter 5 of *Huck Finn*. All available evidence suggests that Jimmy Finn hastened his own inglorious demise in 1845, when Sam was nine, by selling his body to one of the local sawbones for whiskey money.[26]

At the very least, the presence in Hannibal of slavery and the meatpacking plants when Sam was a boy should dispel the myth of the bucolic village, the idyllic "white town drowsing in the sunshine" of "Old Times on the Mississippi" or the allegorical "Delectable Land" of *Tom Sawyer*.[27] Not until 1851, with the start of construction on the Hannibal and St. Joseph Railroad along the river, was Bear Creek finally covered through town, becoming an underground sewer. While Sam may have depicted his hometown through a haze of nostalgia as the near-idyllic St. Petersburg in *Tom Sawyer*, he portrayed it in increasingly realistic terms during the course of his career: as Guilford in *Simon Wheeler, Detective* (ca. 1877), Bricksville in *Huck Finn*, Camelot in *A Connecticut Yankee*, Dawson's Landing in *The Tragedy of Pudd'nhead Wilson* (1894), Hadleyburg in "The Man That Corrupted Hadleyburg" (1899), Eseldorf (or ass-town) in "The Chronicle of Young Satan" version of *The Mysterious Stranger* (1900), and Indiantown in "What Was It?" (1903). In what Henry Nash Smith has called "the matter of Hannibal," as in many other literary trends during his career, Sam was ahead of the curve. He pioneered the so-called revolt from the village over a generation before Edgar Lee Master's *Spoon River Anthology* (1915), Sherwood Anderson's *Winesburg, Ohio* (1919), and Sinclair Lewis's *Main Street* (1920).

Then there was the grinding poverty of Sam's hardscrabble boyhood. "In the small town of Hannibal, Missouri, when I was a boy, everybody was poor, but didn't know it," he remembered in 1890, because "everybody was comfortable." Not necessarily. He readily allowed elsewhere that "the class lines were quite clearly drawn" in the village—that is, some families were less equal than others, particularly the white-trash, dirt-poor Blankenships, who lived in a ramshackle, barnlike building behind the Clemens home on Hill Street and were effectively ostracized by respectable folks. The paterfamilias, Woodson Blankenship, was a peckerwood from South Carolina, another one of the models for Muff Potter in *Tom Sawyer*. In the Hannibal of Sam's childhood, the position of town drunk was practically an elected office. In 1845, when Sam was nine, the elder Blankenship's name appeared on the roll of tax delinquents. Much as Huck's mother is absent from all the stories in which he appears, moreover, Mother Blankenship is never explicitly mentioned in any of Sam's reminiscences about the family; in "Villagers of 1840–3" he merely notes in passing that the parents were "paupers and drunkards." The oldest son Bence was "a hard case with certain good traits,"[28] including his charity toward the fugitive slave Neriam Todd. He earned the family livelihood by fishing.

Bence's younger brother Tom Blankenship was "a kindly young heathen." That is, he was exactly like Huck, an urchin and juvenile pariah. As Paine reported, he was "a ruin of rags, a river-rat, an irresponsible bit of human drift, kind of heart and possessing that priceless boon, absolute unaccountability of conduct to any living soul." Tom, "ignorant, unwashed, insufficiently fed," was also the envy of all the other boys because as an outcast and untouchable he was "the only really independent person" in the village. Younger than Ben Clemens but four years older than Sam, Tom Blankenship "was a good boy, notwithstanding his circumstances," Sam averred in 1906. "To my mind he was a better boy" than a pair of "swells of the ancient days" put together:

Henry Beebe, the son of the slave trader, and John or Jim Reagan, another model for the "new boy" in *Tom Sawyer*, whose family had moved to Hannibal from St. Louis. Because there was no free public education in the village at the time, none of the nine Blankenship ragamuffins attended school—another reason they were envied by the other children. Not that Tom Blankenship lived an altogether enviable life. He spent most of the winter of 1861, when he was thirty years old and Sam was silver mining in Nevada, in the county lockup for stealing turkeys. Though Sam heard that Tom eventually moved to Montana and became a judge, the truth is probably much more mundane. He likely died in middle age of cholera in Missouri.[29]

Tom's sisters were no less the victims of their parents' poverty. Sam once insisted that in his hometown "no young girl was ever insulted, or seduced, or even scandalously gossiped about. Such things were not even dreamed of in that society, much less spoken of and referred to as possibilities." He knew better. As he makes clear in "Villagers of 1840–3," he was familiar with adultery, prostitution, child marriage, and acts of rape in the Hannibal of his boyhood. Some of the Blankenship girls were in fact accused of prostitution—"not proven,"[30] Sam hastened to add, though among the businesses in the town before he left in 1853 were a couple of bawdy houses. It was hardly the pastoral village of legend. As early as the fall of 1846 the *Hannibal Gazette* reported on "the fearful inroads that vice, in its worst forms, and all kinds of immorality are making in Hannibal." Years later, upon learning that Tom's sister Becca had died, he noted that she had worked as a housekeeper for a Hannibal family for forty-five years and "was a highly respected lady" and "a member of the Park Methodist Church and a Christian woman." Becca may in fact have been Tom's twin.[31] Eventually, Sam wrote in 1897, the Blankenship family "played out"—the phrase refers to an exhausted mine—"and disappeared."[32]

Even the play of the village children was fraught with danger. Sam claimed that as a child in Hannibal he nearly drowned nine times. He was rescued once by a slave who "plucked me out of Bear Creek by the hair of my head when I was going down for the third time," on another occasion by a slave who worked for a local hotel, and a third time, when he was nine, by a tailor's apprentice. On still another occasion, he recalled that he once "jumped overboard from the ferry boat in the middle of the river" on a stormy day "to get my hat" and "swam two or three miles after it (and *got* it,) while all the town collected on the wharf and for an hour or so looked out across the angry waste of 'whitecaps' toward where people said Sam Clemens was last seen before he went down." Before he returned the townspeople began to fire a cannon to raise his body, an incident he later incorporated into both

Tom Sawyer and *Huckleberry Finn*. His nearest brush with death, however, occurred when he swam across the river near the town of Scipio:

> When I got near the other shore one leg cramped. I crawled up on the bank and rubbed my leg to get the cramps out of it. The sun was going down and the chill of evening was setting in and I had to swim back. After a while I started and when I got halfway across my leg commenced drawing up, then the other began to cramp, but I swam on. Once, when near the shore, I thought I would let down, but was afraid to, knowing that if the water was deep I was a goner, but finally my knees struck the sand and I crawled out. That was the closest call I ever had.

Jane Clemens plucked up her courage, according to her son, and remarked that "people who are born to be hanged are safe in the water." Her warning echoes Jim's advice to Huck: "keep 'way fum de water as much as you kin," even though you "don't run no resk" of drowning "'kase it's down in de bills dat you's gwyne to get hung."[33]

Whether or not Sam nearly drowned nine times, certainly this incident occurred: in August 1847, less than five months after the death of Marshall Clemens, Sam's ten-year-old classmate Clint Levering drowned in the Mississippi while swimming with friends, including eleven-year-old Sam, who tried in vain to rescue him. As he described the accident in *Life on the Mississippi*, Clint (renamed Lem Hackett) "drowned—on a Sunday. He fell out of an empty flat-boat, where he was playing. Being loaded with sin, he went to the bottom like an anvil." In fact, Clint probably drowned on Friday, August 13. Sam changed the day of the week in order to satirize the Sunday school books whose morality required sinful boys who played on the Sabbath to be stricken dead in retribution for their misbehavior. He included this entry in "Villagers of 1840–3": "Clint Levering drowned. His less fortunate brother lived to have a family and be rich and respected." Clint's death also became grist for Sam's literary mill in *Tom Sawyer* when Huck alludes to the drowning of "Bill Turner" the previous summer.[34]

There was yet another childhood mishap: Sam's boyhood chum Tom Nash, a fellow member of the Cadets of Temperance, was injured while skating on the river. He broke through the ice and, though he climbed out, caught a chill, followed by a cold, then scarlet fever, and lost his hearing. He worked for the rest of his life around Hannibal as a house and sign painter, glazier, and paper hanger and became an object of pity. "He is a young man raised in our midst, and we hope our citizens will encourage him. He works *cheap*," the *Hannibal Tri-Weekly Messenger* editorialized in 1856. In "The Chronicle of Young Satan" Sam reimagined Nash in the character of

Nikolaus Bauman who, after a similar accident, suffers an even worse fate: Nikolaus is left "a paralytic log, deaf, dumb, blind, and praying night and day for the blessed relief of death."[35]

Sam also long remembered a boyhood prank that nearly ended in injury or worse. With Will Bowen, John Briggs, and perhaps one or two other boys he dislodged a boulder on Holliday's Hill that

> rolled down the slope, tearing up saplings, mowing bushes down like grass, ripping and crushing and smashing everything in its path—eternally splintered and scattered a wood pile at the foot of the hill, and then sprang from the high bank clear over a dray in the road—the negro glanced up once and dodged—and the next second it made infinitesimal mince-meat of a frame cooper-shop, and the coopers swarmed out like bees. Then we said it was perfectly magnificent, and left. Because the coopers were starting up the hill to inquire.

Sam not only mentioned the prank in *The Innocents Abroad* (1869) but reminisced with Briggs about the incident upon his return to Hannibal a half century later. Briggs remembered that the boys had dug "the dirt out from under [the rock] for three Sundays," and Sam added without a hint of remorse that "if it had killed that negro we would have had a dead negro on our hands with not a cent to pay for him." After the boulder smashed into the cooper's shop, the boys ran home and "played innocents," though "the patroles gave us a close chase."[36]

But of all the acts of violence with which the teenage Sam Clemens was familiar, none compares to the brutal murders in Union Township, twenty-five miles northwest of Hannibal, of ten-year-old Thomas Bright and his twelve-year-old sister Susannah on October 30, 1849. While the children were gathering nuts in the woods near their home, they were assaulted by a slave known as Glascock's Ben, who bludgeoned Thomas to death and raped Susannah before killing her and cutting off her ears and nose with a Barlow knife. The case became a cause célèbre in Marion County. At the trial, the prosecution alleged Glascock's Ben had raped three women in Virginia before he was sold to Thomas Glascock and moved with him to Missouri. The implication was that the Virginia authorities permitted him to be sold and carried out of state because of his value as chattel. Ben was convicted and, as was normal at the time, his execution was a public spectacle. Early in the afternoon of January 11, 1850, he was strung up before a crowd of some five thousand people—the first legal execution in the history of Marion County. Sam may have witnessed the hanging. If so, he never explicitly mentioned it. But he apparently reimagined it in the execution of the murderer Robert

Hardy in his posthumously published sketch "A Curious Scrap of History" (written in 1894), set in a fictionalized Hannibal in the 1840s: "People came from miles around to see the hanging, they brought cakes and cider, also the women and children, and made a picnic of the matter. It was the largest crowd the village had ever seen. The rope that hanged Hardy was eagerly bought up, in inch samples, for everybody wanted a memento of the memorable event."[37]

Whether or not he viewed the execution, Sam certainly was familiar with Ben's crimes. The transcript of the trial in Palmyra was splashed over the first two pages of Ament's *Missouri Courier* for December 6, 1849, and Ben's confession to the crimes while walking to the gallows was printed in the paper six weeks later and subsequently reprinted in pamphlet form. Ben admitted that he thought his life would be spared because, like Tom Driscoll in *Pudd'nhead Wilson*, he was precious property. In any event, Sam alluded to Ben's atrocities in chapter 29 of *Tom Sawyer* when Injun Joe orders a confederate to mutilate Widow Douglas: "You slit her nostrils—you notch her ears like a sow!" (In the original manuscript, his command is even more striking: "You cut her nose off—and her ears.") Sam referred again to Glascock's Ben in "Villagers of 1840–3" as "the hanged nigger" who "raped and murdered a girl . . . in the woods." As late as 1901, over a half century after the gruesome crimes, Sam solicited information about the incident from his publisher because he was planning a story based on it in which Tom and Huck rescue the children. He could not remember names but, as he noted, the culprit "raped a young girl and clubbed her and her young brother to death. It was in Marion County, Missouri."[38]

One other dimension to the case of Glascock's Ben is worth mentioning. On October 26, 1849, Thomas Hart Benton, U.S. senator from Missouri, spoke in Hannibal while campaigning for reelection. He was engaged in the political fight of his life. He had announced his opposition to slavery earlier that year and his political enemies in the state, where politics was both a form of entertainment and a contact sport, accused him of "free soil" sympathies. Sam mentions Benton in chapter 22 of *Tom Sawyer*: "the greatest man in the world (as Tom supposed), Mr. Benton, an actual United States Senator, proved an overwhelming disappointment—for he was not twenty-five feet high." Ament was even more disappointed. A rabidly proslavery Democrat, he filled the *Missouri Courier* with invective denouncing Benton, including one article titled "Benton's Speech—The Dictator in the Ditch."[39] Whatever traction Benton may have earned with his campaign appearance in Hannibal dissipated four days later with the murder of the Bright children by a criminal slave. Benton was defeated in his bid for reelection, and he never again served in the Senate.

◈

Despite his poor health as an infant, Sam was a robust adolescent. With the exception of the time he had the measles, he bragged at his seventieth birthday celebration in 1905 that "I have seldom taken a dose of medicine, and have still seldomer needed one." To be sure, he suffered from chilblains every winter from the age of five until early adulthood, when he cured them with kerosene, a toxic allopathic remedy. Luckily, he escaped the yellow fever epidemic in 1849–50 that threatened, according to his mother, to "depopulate the town," and also the annual cholera epidemics along the river, though eventually he became bedridden with the disease while living in St. Louis in 1853. When he was ill, Jane Clemens doctored him with home remedies, "glorified quack-poisons," and patented medicines such as Perry Davis's Pain-Killer, a tonic that contained alcohol, camphor, capsicum, gum myrrh, and gum opium,[40] the same nostrum Aunt Polly administers to the hero and Tom to the family cat in *Tom Sawyer*.

Sam also drank Mississippi River water for its purported medicinal benefits, a variation on the custom of clay eating practiced in the South. "People who drink it never like to drink any other [water]," he said. Unlike the clear water of the Ohio River, the Big Muddy was wholesome and nutritious, according to folk belief, "and a man that drank Mississippi water could grow corn in his stomach if he wanted to." The "good alluvial loam" would "line you inside with more aluminum than would otherwise be the case." Every tumbler of the father of waters "holds nearly an acre of land in solution," Sam joked in *Life on the Mississippi*, and if you "let your glass stand half an hour, you can separate the land from the water as easy as Genesis; and then you will find them both good: the one good to eat, the other good to drink. The land is very nourishing, the water is thoroughly wholesome. The one appeases hunger; the other, thirst." Charles Dickens drank Mississippi River water—what he dubbed "liquid mud" during his North American speaking tour in 1842—and, he remarked in *American Notes*, "It is considered wholesome by the natives, and is something more opaque than gruel. I have seen water like it at the filter-shops, but nowhere else."[41]

The treatment of mental illness in Hannibal during Sam's childhood was more medieval than modern. He was familiar with at least two cases. Elizabeth Campbell Bowen, sister of the Bowen brothers, was mentally disabled from birth and suffered her entire life from neglect. Sam described her plight in chapter 53 of *Life on the Mississippi*. Startled one night by a girl who carried a skull and "wore a shroud and a doughface," Eliza had "looked up and screamed, and then fell into convulsions"; she "went mad" and "never got a shred of her mind back." She spent "[t]hirty-six years in a madhouse" so that "some young fools might have some fun!" In August 1876 Will Bowen wrote Sam that his sister had finally died "in the Asylum." Sam subsequently considered incorporating the incident into a Huck-Tom sequel he never wrote in which a young girl "made up a skull and doughface into an apparition and so frightened an old woman that she went crazy."

Then there was the son of one of the local physicians, James Ratcliff, who lived in chains in a shed behind the family home: "Fed through a hole. Would not wear clothes, winter or summer. Could not have fire. . . . Believed his left hand had committed a mortal sin," so he "chopped it off." He became the model for the character of Crazy Meadows, "a slender, tall, wild-looking man" in the "Schoolhouse Hill" version of *The Mysterious Stranger*.[42]

There was one hazard Sam fortunately never faced: the barbarity of Injun Joe, depicted in *Tom Sawyer* as the locus of all evil in St. Petersburg. Injun Joe Douglass was in fact an innocuous figure, employed by the Fuqua family and others in the village as a man of all work. He was a mestizo, part Mexican and part Osage or Cherokee, and he had apparently survived a scalping as a teenager in Oklahoma before arriving in Hannibal in the early 1850s. He lived in a hollow tree on Bear Creek and, according to Barney Farthing, he "was a great friend of the boys." In his only nonfictional reference to Joe, Sam simply remarked that he was one of the "intemperate ne'er-do-wells in Hannibal."[43] Certainly he was not the hellhound portrayed in *Tom Sawyer*.

In the spring of 1849 Hannibal became a way station to the West, a crossroads during the Gold Rush. It was "just far enough north to be where West was South and East was North," James M. Cox once explained. A decade earlier, six-day-per-week steamboat service had been established during the summer months between Keokuk, Iowa, sixty-five miles north of Hannibal, and St. Louis, about a hundred miles south as the buzzard flies, with travel connections to all points on the compass. By 1846 three steamboats on average stopped in Hannibal every day, a total of 1,080 during the year. "All emigrants went through there," Sam noted. Over two hundred Hannibal citizens rushed to California after the discovery of gold, about eighty of them in the spring of 1849. Among them were Bill Briggs (John's brother); Sam's former teacher Sam Cross; his former classmate Reuel Gridley; Ben Hawkins (Laura's brother); Benjamin Horr (Elizabeth's brother); Hugh Meredith, the Clemens family physician, and his son Charles; Neil Moss (Mary's brother); William Owsley; and Sam's cousin Jim Quarles. The next year, Archibald Robards—a local entrepreneur who owned a flour mill, a machine shop and foundry, a hotel, and slaves and was one of the elders in the Campbellite church and its most generous benefactor—led a group of fifteen men, including his son John, Sam's schoolmate, to California via New Mexico. "I remember the departure of the cavalcade when it spurred westward," Sam remembered over a half century later. "We were all there to see and to envy." As Jane and Pamela informed Orion in late January 1850, "Nearly all those who went from here last spring have written back that they are making large fortunes." Others were not so lucky: Melicent Holliday became a widow after her husband Richard, for whom Holliday's Hill is named, joined the exodus and died in California. A half century later, Sam condemned the "Californian rush for wealth" for the change it wrought in the nation. It "begot the lust for money which is the rule of life to-day, and the hardness and cynicism which is the spirit of to-day."[44] But when he traveled west to the mining camps in 1861 he was no less culpable, ironically, than the hoards he condemned for succumbing to the sound of the chink of gold.

The Gold Rush also funneled a steady stream of vagrants and varmints through the village. Barney Farthing recalled that "every day during the spring and summer" of 1849 and 1850 "long trains of canvas covered wagons, drawn by horses, mules, or oxen" passed through Hannibal. "Long processions of big whiskered men, wearing red shirts, blue jeans trousers, and high top boots, carrying at shoulder or belt, guns, pistols, and big butcher knives, rode or walked beside these trains." Sam remembered in particular a "young California emigrant who was stabbed with the bowie knife by a drunken comrade: I saw the red life gush from his breast"—probably the murder in a local saloon reported in the *Hannibal Courier* on April 11, 1850. Injun Joe's threats to the Widow Douglas are also likely based on an actual incident in May 1850, when a young Californian passing through the town shouted "coarse challenges and obscenities" at the door of the Widow Weir, who shot and killed him. Sam also recalled, both in interviews and his autobiography, how the boys in his gang "used to dig in the little plot" at the mouth of Mc-Dowell's Cave "in emulation of the Forty-niners, who were passing through our town. We'd keep an account of the gold we dug every day,"[45] much as he mined for precious metals in Nevada in 1861–62 and much as Tom and Huck hunt for buried treasure in chapters 25–26 of *Tom Sawyer*.

Explored in 1819 by a hunter named Jack Simms and located some two miles downriver from Bear Creek, the limestone labyrinth was called Simms's Cave or Saltpeter Cave by the whites in the region before it was purchased by Dr. Joseph Nash McDowell—a rabid Southerner, prominent St. Louis physician, and founder of the first medical school in the city—and renamed McDowell's Cave. While privately owned, it was open to the public until late 1845, when McDowell sealed it with an iron or oaken door so that he could stockpile munitions, either to support an American military

invasion of Mexico or to repel a Mexican invasion of the American Southwest. In fact, several dozen men from the Hannibal region had joined the
army to fight in Mexico—including "Honest John" Hawkins and his son
Ben, the father and brother of Sam's sweetheart Laura Hawkins—and had
bivouacked in Santa Fe. After the Mexican-American War ended in 1848,
McDowell unbarred the door and again opened it to visitors—with a twist.
He permitted a relative, Dr. E. D. McDowell, to install a sarcophagus, a
copper cylinder filled with alcohol containing the body of his fourteen-year-
old daughter, in the cave. He believed the body would eventually mummify
like the bodies of several Indians who had been found in the saltpeter caves
of Kentucky. But as Sam explained in *Life on the Mississippi*, "The top of the
cylinder was removable; and it was said to be a common thing for the baser
order of tourists to drag the dead face into view and examine it and comment
upon it."[46] Given the threat of vandalism, McDowell was compelled to re-
move and bury the body after only three or four years. Over the next decade,
the cave reportedly sheltered escaped slaves on the Underground Railroad,
and when the Civil War erupted McDowell may have again cached weapons
there for the Confederate Army. At the end of the century, Jesse James may
have used it as a hideout.

But in the late 1840s the "great Missouri labyrinth" was a favorite rec-
reation site for local residents. Both Laura Hawkins and Orion in his final
Lorio letter to the *St. Louis Reveille* mention picnics there. "Usually my elder
sister" and Sam's sister Pamela, Laura recalled, accompanied them "to see
that we didn't get lost among the winding passages where our candles lighted
up the great stalagmites and stalactites, and where water was dripping from
the stone roof overhead." The boys in town also used it as a hideout, though
at the time it had been only partially mapped and some erstwhile explorers,
according to local legend, had starved to death in its depths. Orion speculat-
ed in 1847 that it was "at least eight or ten square miles" in extent. In 1852,
in one of the first pieces he wrote for publication outside Hannibal, Sam
reported that the cave was "of unknown length; it has innumerable passages,
which are not unlike the streets of a large city. The ceiling arches over, and
from it hang beautiful stalactites, which sparkle in the light of the torches,
and remind one of the fairy palaces spoken of in the Arabian Nights. There
are several springs, rivers, and wells, some of which are of unknown depth."
In the final chapters of *Tom Sawyer*, Tom and Becky become lost in McDougal's Cave, the name given "the vast labyrinth of crooked aisles" in the novel.
"It was said," Sam wrote in the novel, "that one might wander days and nights
together through its intricate tangle of rifts and chasms, and never find the
end of the cave; and that he might go down, and down, and still down, into

the earth, and it was just the same—labyrinth under labyrinth, and no end to any of them. No man 'knew' the cave. That was an impossible thing."

The Hannibal boys explored it anyway, according to Barney Farthing. One day in 1850, two years after the end of the Mexican-American War and a few months after the corpse of the McDowell girl was moved to the family plot in St. Louis, the intrepid band of boys gathered "at our rendezvous, the foot of Lover's Leap," south of town on a direct route to the cavern. Like Tom at the head of Tom Sawyer's Gang, Sam was the "self-appointed and undisputed leader" of the group on these excursions. In addition to Sam and Barney, the group included Tom Blankenship; Bob Bodine, who nearly forty years later would become a U.S. congressman from Missouri; John Briggs; George Butler, the nephew of the Civil War general Ben "Beast" Butler; and John Meredith. They were outfitted with "purloined candles and horse pistols that were too rusty to fire." The upshot of the expedition was that the boys became lost in the cave for thirty hours, much as Tom and Becky become lost after the school picnic. During the night they spent belowground, according to Farthing, "all of us recalled" the stories about folks who had died in the cave. "Finally we fell asleep, sobbing." They were rescued by a search party the next day.[47]

In the summer of 1850 Orion left St. Louis to edit a weekly paper in Hannibal, a move he had been contemplating for several months. The telegraph had arrived in Hannibal in September 1849, wiring the town to the rest of the world, so the moment seemed propitious. As early as January 1850 he apparently invited Sam to join him in the venture, though his brother hung fire. "Sam says he can't leave Ament," Jane notified Orion. Sam intended "to make him pay wages" after his apprenticeship ended "and you would want him to wait." She urged Orion to find some St. Louis investors to purchase the paper for him. "I think about the time you come up they will be through and you can get it at your own way. I think if you could get some of the printers in St. L[ouis] that are doing well to buy the of[fice] and give you an intrust [interest] let you come up and take charge of the office, get some old person to assist a little in editing merely to have their name." He could employ his twelve-year-old brother Henry as a printer's devil, and she "could board the hands." In February, Henry acknowledged in a letter to Orion that "if you come and buy the Journal office" he would apprentice with him. In April, Jane advised Orion that J. S. Buchanan had put the *Hannibal Journal* up for sale. That same month Orion contacted a New York real estate agent and offered to sell parcels of the Tennessee land for ten cents an acre through his agency and the next month he received fifty dollars for a section.

This money, in addition to five hundred dollars he borrowed at an exorbitant rate of interest from his distant cousin John Moorman Johnson, a Baptist minister and farmer who lived near Hannibal, enabled Orion to buy a hand-press and type and to move his family from the second floor of Grant's Drug Store back across Hill Street into the clapboard house his father had built. Jane took in a few boarders, including Orion's apprentices, to help make ends meet. "She used the provisions I supplied her," Orion recalled. "We therefore had a regular diet of bacon, butter, bread, and coffee."[48]

The first issue of the weekly Hannibal *Western Union*—the title betrays Orion's political sympathies—appeared on September 5. In his prospectus for the paper, Orion declared that as "a thorough Whig" his "political articles will bear the genuine whig stamp," but he vowed that "no effort will be spared to obtain for the public the very latest news, on all subjects" and that he would impart to the paper "a high degree of interest and usefulness to every class of readers." A subscription cost two dollars a year, payable in advance, and a twelve-line classified ad a dollar. Orion accepted farm produce and cordwood in lieu of cash. He ran the paper on a shoestring, in part by engaging two apprentices, his brother Henry and a "green, good-natured, bashful" country boy some five years older than Henry named Jim Wolf, who wanted to learn the trade and worked for room and board. Wolf later became the butt of Sam's practical jokes and, in his autobiography, he expressed regret for his behavior. His ruses had been "all cruel and all barren of wit. Any brainless swindler could have invented them," whereas Wolf "brought all his native sweetnesses and gentlenesses and simplicities with him." He was "always tongue-tied in the presence of my sister, and when even my gentle mother spoke to him he could not answer save in frightened monosyllables." Wolf appears in *A Tramp Abroad* (1880) in the role of the "loose-jointed, long-legged, tow-headed, jeans-clad countrified" raconteur Nicodemus Dodge.[49]

In the fragmented political landscape of the early 1850s, Orion threaded a needle in his editorials because he could not risk alienating his readers and advertisers. He may have been opposed to slavery, but he was equally critical of Southern fire-eaters and Northern abolitionists. A conservative Whig, he attacked Free-Soilers and never editorially condemned involuntary servitude. He defended the Compromise of 1850 and the Fugitive Slave Act as measures necessary for the preservation of the Union. His paper carried advertisements for runaway slaves and slave sales, on the one hand, and for a colonization paper, the *Christian Statesman*, on the other. As Philip Fanning notes, Orion "rebuked alike the Northern radicals who obstructed the enforcement of the Fugitive Slave Law and their counterparts in the South who openly called for secession." He took no side in theological debates, moreover, except to express disapproval of the Latter-Day Saints, whose capital was located in Nauvoo, Illinois, only sixty miles upstream from Hannibal, where Joseph Smith was killed in 1844. As Orion put it, Mormons were "about as tractable and peaceable as so many grizzly bears."[50] Meanwhile, he fended off his local competitors, including Joe Buchanan's *Hannibal Journal*, William League and J. T. Hinton's *Whig Messenger*, and Ament's *Missouri Courier*.

Orion finally lured Sam away from Ament's shop in January 1851 by promising him a salary of $3.50 a week. It was "an extravagant wage," Sam remembered in his autobiography, "but Orion was always generous, always liberal with everybody except himself." Besides, the promise "cost him nothing in my case, for he never was able to pay me a single penny as long as I was with him."[51] In effect, Sam became an unpaid apprentice like Henry Clemens and Jim Wolf. But Orion was the breadwinner, the sole support of the family, and for the first time in their lives all three surviving Clemens brothers worked side by side.

On January 9, a few days after Sam joined the *Western Union* staff, a fire broke out in the plant on Bird Street. Sam lampooned Wolf's response to the fire in his first known writing, "A Gallant Fireman," a 150-word squib in the January 16 issue of the paper. Edgar Marquess Branch speculates that it was "produced by the young compositor while he stood at his case setting it into type." It was not an auspicious start to a literary career. With the building on fire, Sam explained, Wolf had "immediately gathered the broom, an old mallet, the wash-pan and a dirty towel" and run some ten blocks with them. By the time he returned the fire had been doused, at which point he uttered a malapropism: "If that thar fire hadn't bin put out, thar'd a' bin the greatest *confirmation* of the age!"[52]

After the fire, Orion moved the handpress to a room over Stover & Horr's Clothing Store on Main Street and soldiered on. The *Western Union* was issued without interruption the following week. With an additional five hundred dollars borrowed from John Moorman Johnson, Orion bought the *Hannibal Journal* (and a piano) in late summer from Buchanan, who promptly vamoosed for California, and merged the two papers. The first weekly issue of the consolidated *Hannibal Journal and Western Union* appeared on September 4, 1851—the title would soon be shortened to the *Hannibal Journal*—and Orion bragged that it had "a larger circulation, by *over one hundred*," than any other paper in the region.

About the same time, according to Sam, Orion "was hit a staggering blow by a new idea—an idea that had never been thought of in the West by any person before—the idea of hiring a literary celebrity to write an original story for his Hannibal newspaper *for pay!*" He wanted a tale "which could be continued through three issues of his weekly paper and cover a few columns of solid bourgeois each time. He offered a sum to all the American literary celebrities of that day" but "Emerson, Lowell, Holmes, and all the others declined." (There is no evidence other than this singular statement by Sam that Orion contacted any of these distinguished men of letters, or if he did that any of them replied.) Finally, "a celebrity of about the third degree took him up—with a condition." He would not write "an original story for the sum offered—*which was five dollars*—but would translate one from the French for that sum. My brother took him up" and "the story came."[53] Published without signature in three successive issues of the newspaper, on September 25 and October 2 and 9, 1851, the science fiction tale "More Wonderful Still!" was translated from French "expressly for the *Hannibal Journal and Western Union*," the headnote trumpeted.[54]

After the merger of the *Journal* and *Western Union*, Orion reduced the subscription price of the paper from two dollars to one dollar a year "and the advertising rates in about the same proportion," Sam recalled, in hopes of boosting circulation, attracting more advertisers, and increasing net profit. Instead, the strategy backfired. As Sam wisecracked, he instead "created one absolute and unassailable certainty—to wit: that the business would never pay him a single cent of profit." Orion repeatedly flirted with disaster. Twice within a six-week period in early 1852, on January 22 and March 2, the *Journal* offices again caught fire. The first time, both Ament and William League of the *Messenger* assisted the *Journal* staff in producing the next issue of the paper in their shops. Orion eventually collected about $150 in insurance money. The second time the blaze was much larger. It consumed Garth's tobacco factory adjacent to the *Journal* office, a loss totaling about five thousand dollars. Ament helped move the *Journal* handpress, paper, and type across the street before they were destroyed. Afterward, Orion slashed expenses and, rather than pay office rent, moved the entire *Journal* operation into the Clemens house. Still, some indications of Orion's financial distress were evident as early as June 1852, when he postponed his plans to enlarge the paper and warned subscribers that his carriers would try to collect money owed him. "He kept that paper alive during four years," Sam remembered, "but I have at this time no idea how he accomplished it." Ament performed yet another favor for him when in November 1852 he sold his interest in the *Missouri Courier* and moved to Palmyra, where he soon was rewarded for his party service by appointment as receiver of the U.S. Land Office by President Franklin Pierce. Orion congratulated his old rival: he was "a clever man and a man of strict integrity. . . . Although he has given us some hard raps for what he was pleased to call our 'rabid whiggery,' yet we are willing to render justice to a political opponent."[55]

Like many another country editor, Orion weathered the storm by filling his news columns and feuilleton with material culled from his exchanges. In the age before the telegraph and wire services, the flow of information was facilitated by a system of gifting through the mail. The Postal Service Act of 1792 authorized presses to exchange free copies of their newspapers and magazines without a postage fee. Among the exchanges sent to the *Hannibal Journal* were the Boston *Carpet-Bag* (a short-lived humor magazine edited by B. P. Shillaber), *Godey's Lady's Book*, *Knickerbocker*, the Boston *Olive Branch*, *Peterson's*, *Sartain's*, *Scientific American*, and *Spirit of the Times*. Articles from all of them were copied occasionally in the *Journal*. In the absence of international copyright or even an effective domestic copyright law, moreover, Orion reprinted for free works by such authors as Sylvanus Cobb Jr., the elder Alexandre Dumas, Fanny Fern, Oliver Optic, and the humorist Josh Silsbee. He reproduced Charles Dickens's story "The Fate of a Drunkard" and an excerpt from *Bleak House* at about the same time he encouraged Sam to read Dickens. ("I was ashamed, but I couldn't do it," Sam admitted.) One of the first issues Sam helped to typeset included an article about the "rapping" Fox sisters, who gained wide fame as spiritual mediums—years before they revealed that they had made the sounds at their séances by cracking their toes under a table. The *Journal* also reprinted columns by the travel writer J. Ross Browne—this a decade before Sam befriended Browne in California. No doubt Sam read, if he did not typeset, a piece in the *Hannibal Journal* in November 1852, copied from the London papers, describing a new "method of finding drowned persons" by filling a loaf of bread with quicksilver or mercury and floating it on the water, where it ostensibly would settle over a decomposing body. Sam later alluded to precisely this practice in both *Tom Sawyer* and *Huckleberry Finn*. If, as Herman Melville's Ishmael declares, the whaleship was his Harvard and Yale, then the print shop was Sam's Columbia and Princeton; and indeed Abraham Lincoln once called the printing house "the poor boy's college." By typesetting "acres of good and bad literature," Sam learned over time—"unconsciously at first, consciously later—to discriminate between the two." As a result, he worked to polish his style. In addition to Sam, such distinguished writers as Benjamin Franklin, Bret Harte, W. D. Howells, and Walt Whitman all worked in early life as printers. Harte, for one, remembered how the discipline of composing at the case shaped his writing. He learned "to combine the composition of the editorial with the setting of its type" and "to save my fingers mechanical drudgery somewhat condensed my style."[56]

Sam turned his familiarity with the *Carpet-Bag* to advantage when, at the age of seventeen, he sent its editors the manuscript of "The Dandy Frightening the Squatter," a crude anecdote depicting the confrontation of an eastern dude and a Pike County frontiersman. It appeared in the May 1, 1852, issue alongside sketches by the popular humorists Charles Farrar Browne (aka Artemus Ward) and George Horatio Derby (aka John Phoenix). The publication is remarkable for a couple of reasons. Sam's submission to a nationally circulated comic paper betrays, as David E. E. Sloane has noted, "a measurable degree of literary ambition" in the teenager, and the joke exhibits all the characteristics of Southwestern humor, including not merely the defeat but the humiliation of the victim. The victor adds insult to injury. Coarse as it is, it also enjoyed a long shelf life. Signed "S.L.C." and set in Hannibal, it was copied from the *Carpet-Bag* at least seven times over the next few years in newspapers from Nyack, New York, to Palmyra, Missouri. Sam also contributed a pair of articles to the Philadelphia *American Courier* in 1852, including "Hannibal, Missouri," in which he mentioned "the crystal waters of the proud Mississippi"[57]—a surprising reference to a river well known for its chocolate-brown color.

In chapter 51 of *Life on the Mississippi*, Sam observed that when he was a schoolboy in Hannibal "a couple of young Englishmen came to the town and sojourned a while; and one day they got themselves up in cheap royal finery and did the Richard III swordfight with maniac energy and prodigious pow-wow, in the presence of the village boys." No doubt he refers to the performance of a couple of confidence men in March 1852. They advertised their appearance at Benton Hall in the *Hannibal Journal* on March 11, and the next issue, dated March 18, contained a review of the production that fleshes out details:

> Last week a profusion of bills, ornamenting the hotels and sides of prominent buildings, announced that the above "*celebrated*" troupe were going to perform certain specified wonders at Benton Hall. All the little boys in town gazed on the groups of astonishing pictures which appeared on the above mentioned bills and were thereby wrought up to an intense pitch of excitement. It was to be a real theatre, and the "troupe," (which nobody had ever heard of before,) was so "celebrated." Well, the momentous evening came. Those who enjoyed the felicity of paying a quarter to see the show found a large man on the first story, who received the money, and a small man at the top of the second pair of steps, who received the tickets. These men, thus engaged in this apparently humble occupation, were the very persons who were afterwards transformed into heroes and soldiers by the power of paint. In the hall we found forty or fifty of our citizens, sitting in front of a striped curtain, behind which was all the mysterious paraphernalia of the theatre.

When the curtain was pulled to one side, the first appearance on the stage was the large man who received the money at the top of the first pair of stairs. He was evidently a novice, and acted his part about as you have seen boys, in a thespian society. He was intended to be a lover of the distinguished danseuse, who played the part of a miss in short dresses, though her apparent age would have justified her in wearing them longer, and we have seen spectacles on younger looking people. Then the small man, who came in first as a corporal in the army, and then pretended to be drunk, for the amusement of the audience, made up the third character in this burlesque of a farce, the dullness of which was not relieved even by the disgusting blackguardisms with which it was profusely interlarded.

After this wretched abomination was finished, the danseuse favored the audience with several dances, very skillfully performed, and the only part of the whole performance which was worth going half a square to see, if the charge had been nothing.[58]

Afterward the two frauds disappeared into the Missouri night without a trace, no doubt to lie low until they played the next town.

Sam likely did not write this notice; it was almost certainly penned by Orion. But even if Sam was not the author, he may have set it in type and he undoubtedly witnessed the performance. Over thirty years later, the scam became the basis for the antics of the Duke and King in chapters 20–22 of *Adventures of Huckleberry Finn* in which a pair of unnamed con artists, not that their names matter, "sell" the gullible audience. Like the actual frauds who performed in Hannibal, one of them cross-dresses, and the other is a "novice"; they advertise with handbills; and they charge a quarter per person to attend the show. In chapter 21, the Duke and King similarly rehearse the swordfight from Richard III with "a couple of long swords that the duke made out of oak laths."[59] In a passage deleted from *Life on the Mississippi*, moreover, Sam remembered that one of the charlatans delivered a crack-brained version of Hamlet's soliloquy like the one declaimed by the Duke in *Huck Finn*. Sam embellished their appearances in *Huck Finn* (e.g., by depicting the King's rollicking performance of "the Royal Nonesuch") but he gleaned all the elements of the fictional episode from an actual event.

Another affair during Sam's typesetting days on the *Hannibal Journal* left a lasting impression on him. On Saturday evening, January 23, 1853, he met a stranger, Dennis McDermid or McDavid, a "harmless whisky-sodden tramp" who was "begging for a match" on the chilly streets of the village. Sam fetched him a box, "then hied me home and to bed." Around midnight

the town marshal arrested McDermid "for breaking down the door of a negro cabin with an ax" and locked the tramp in the small jail or calaboose near
the mouth of Bear Creek. At three or four in the morning, "the church bells
rang for fire and everybody turned out," including Sam. McDermid had set
his straw bed on fire and ignited the woodwork of the jail. When he reached
the site of the jail, Sam remembered,

> two hundred men, women, and children stood massed together, transfixed with
> horror, and staring at the grated windows of the jail. Behind the iron bars, and
> tugging frantically at them, and screaming for help, stood the tramp; he seemed
> like a black object set against a sun, so white and intense was the light at his
> back. That marshal could not be found, and he had the only key. A battering-
> ram was quickly improvised, and the thunder of its blows upon the door had so
> encouraging a sound that the spectators broke into wild cheering, and believed
> the merciful battle won. But it was not so. The timbers were too strong; they
> did not yield. It was said that the man's death-grip still held fast to the bars
> after he was dead; and that in this position the fires wrapped him about and
> consumed him. As to this, I do not know. What was seen after I recognized the
> face that was pleading through the bars was seen by others, not by me.

Sam was tortured "for a long time afterward" by the thought that he was "as
guilty of the man's death as if I had given him the matches purposely that he
might burn himself up with them. I had not a doubt that I should be hanged
if my connection with this tragedy were found out."[60] He worried that if he
talked in his sleep his brother Henry would learn his secret.

Orion improved the occasion by editorializing on temperance in the next
issue of his paper and inadvertently rubbing salt in Sam's wound in another
article his brother may have set in type. He implied that the fire in the calaboose was no accident, but divine retribution for sin:

> This man was an insane Irishman—made insane by liquor. . . . It is supposed
> he set his bed clothes on fire with matches, as he usually carried them in his
> pocket to light his pipe. . . . Attempts were made to obtain the keys, and also
> to break down the doors, both of which proved unavailing. The Marshal, who
> has charge of the keys, slept four or five squares distant, and though the keys
> were always kept in one place in the Recorder's office, known to one or two
> others, in the hurry and confusion they were overlooked in the search. Before
> they were obtained, the fire had progressed so rapidly as already to have de-
> stroyed the man's life. Every effort was made to rescue him. To those outside
> endeavoring to force an entrance, he seemed to be leaning against the door,
> shrieking and moaning, until, stifled by the smoke and heated air, he fell to
> the floor.

McDermid had been employed by John Moorman Johnson—coincidentally, the same farmer who had loaned Orion the money to buy his newspaper—and had "proved himself a very good-hearted, clever, honest man." He had left Johnson the previous spring to work on the plank road under construction between Hannibal and New London, but

> indulged in drinking too freely, and lost his senses. For several months past, he seems to have had on him a kind of perpetual delirium tremens. A few pieces of burnt flesh and bones were gathered from the ruins, deposited in a box, and interred in the city burying ground. Thus, living and dying alone and friendless, he suffered in life, met a tragic death, and at last sleeps in a grave that no man honors.

Sam reminisced with Will Bowen in 1870 about "that poor fellow in the calaboose" whom "we accidentally burned up," and he evoked his memory of McDermid in chapter 23 of *Tom Sawyer*. After Muff Potter is falsely accused of Dr. Robinson's murder and jailed, Huck and Tom slip him "some tobacco and matches" through the cell grating and his "gratitude for their gifts . . . smote their consciences."[61] Fortunately, art failed to imitate life. Potter does not use the matches to burn down the jail. (Of course, had Potter died in a jail fire like McDermid, then Sam could not have portrayed his trial in the novel.)

The next month a celebrated fugitive slave case with links to Hannibal came to a head. Jerry McReynolds, an escaped slave belonging to John McReynolds of Marion County, was discovered in October 1851 living in Syracuse, New York, where he had worked as a carpenter for several years. In a vain attempt to enforce the Fugitive Slave Act, the authorities arrested him and planned to return him to his owner in Missouri, but an outraged mob stormed the courthouse jail and freed him—this over two years before similar tactics failed to liberate Anthony Burns in Boston. Orion reprinted an article from the *Buffalo Commercial* about the confrontation and commented on it. He complained that there was "a disposition" in Northern cities "hostile to extending to Southern men rights guaranteed to them by the Constitution and laws of the land." That is, Orion supported the Fugitive Slave Act and opposed efforts to subvert it. "Slaveholders may now set it down as an established fact," he added, "that their chance of recovering a fugitive slave is almost as good in Canada, a foreign country, as in the Northern States of the Union." The owner of an escaped slave "may calculate on recovering his lost property, in those States, if at all, at the imminent risk of failure, after incurring heavy expense, and at the hazard of his life." Sam may well again have typeset his brother's editorial. In any event, he could hardly have been oblivious to the controversy. Sixteen months later, the two dozen abolitionists who incited the "riot" stood trial in Albany, New York, and Orion reprinted an article critical of them from the *Albany State Register*, which claimed that the abolitionists had committed a "high handed outrage" in Syracuse in the course of "one of their fanatical orgies." They were not, however, genuinely sympathetic to Jerry's plight in the opinion of the editorialist. "Having effected their object—excitement, agitation, and a heinous and indictable offence against the laws and the Constitution of the United States," or so went the argument, "they turn the cold shoulder to their penniless victims, and leave them to shift for themselves as best they can. This is a perfect illustration of the character of abolition fanatics."[62] Orion reprinted this piece in the *Journal* without comment, though he doubtless shared the sentiment.

In September 1851 Pamela became the first of the Clemens siblings to marry. She wed William Anderson Moffett, a former Hannibal resident and a prosperous St. Louis merchant, the head of the commission business Moffett, Stillwell, & Co., whose offices in 1859 were located next to the Boggs & U. S. Grant real estate agency on Locust Street. Pamela became pregnant within a few days of the wedding and bore a daughter she and Will named Annie exactly forty weeks later. In his autobiography, Sam remembered Moffett as "a merchant, a Virginian—a fine man in every way." As for his sister Pamela, the model for Tom's cousin Mary in *Tom Sawyer*, she was "a good woman, familiar with grief, though bearing it bravely & giving no sign upon the surface; & she is kind-hearted, void of folly or vanity, perfectly unacquainted with deceit or dissimulation, diffident about her own faults, & slow to discover those of others." He remarked after her death in 1904 that her "character was without blemish, & she was of a most kindly & gentle disposition."[63]

On his part, Sam had plenty of adolescent sweethearts in addition to Laura Hawkins. The first target of his infatuation was probably Mary Miller, who was twice his age and broke his heart by ignoring his suit. But there were other objects of his calf love: Mary Bowen, sister of the Bowen brothers; Jennie Brady, sister of another of Sam's friends; Mary and Artemisia Briggs, sisters of John Briggs; Bettie Ormsley; Arzelia Penn, daughter of one of the founders of the town; Margaret Sexton, whose family briefly boarded at the Clemens house; and Kitty Shoot, daughter of a local hosteler. He may even have briefly been engaged to one of them. According to Sam's niece Annie Moffett, a "young married woman who had formerly lived in Hannibal" once claimed that "she had been engaged" to her uncle. When Annie asked Sam about the truth of her statement, she quoted his reply: "Well, if she says so, it *must* be true." The woman in question likely was Artemisia Briggs, whose marriage in Hannibal to a local bricklayer in March 1853 may have hastened Sam's departure from the village two months later. At any rate, Sam noted in his autobiography in 1906 that Artemisia Briggs "got married not long after refusing me."[64]

Sam learned a few tricks of the advertising trade as a typesetter, too—in particular, how to scream a lead that had nothing to do with the product that was promoted. It was a variation of bait and switch. A long-running ad in the *Hannibal Journal* for a stove store on Main Street, for example, was headlined "Railroad Depot / Located! / It is not yet determined where." Such advertisements inspired Sam's first hoax, a short item in the *Journal* for May 6, 1853: "Terrible Accident! 500 Men Killed and Missing!! We set the above head up, expecting (of course) to use it, but as the accident hasn't happened yet we'll say (To be Continued)."[65] It foreshadowed the type of prank he played many times in the future, especially in advertising his first lectures in California and Nevada.

Sam eventually became the de facto foreman of his brother's shop and, even as a teenager, he wrote items for the paper about violent and broken families. He expressed in his juvenilia a special disgust for husbands who abused

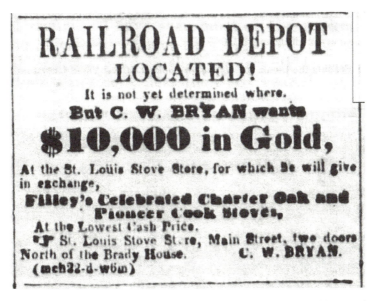

Figure 4. Classified advertisement in the *Hannibal Journal*, April 28, 1853. Collection of Gary Scharnhorst.

their wives. In "A Family Muss," his first substantial article in the *Hannibal Journal*, published on September 9, 1852, under his first pseudonym, W. Epaminondas Adrastus Perkins, he detailed the abusive behavior of a sadistic husband and father. Two months later, in the ironically titled "Connubial Bliss," written shortly before his seventeenth birthday, he referred to the cautionary tales of "bloated, reeling" drunks who sleep "in the gutter at night" and abuse their wives and children by day. The following spring he suggested in the *Journal* that a man guilty of "unmercifully beating and maltreating his wife and children" ought "to be ducked, ridden on a rail, tarred and feathered, and politely requested to bundle up his 'duds' and make himself scarce."[66]

After working for Orion for a year and a half, he seemed ready to assume a larger role in the production of the paper. So when Orion left Hannibal in mid-September 1852 on a two-week business trip to Tennessee to try again to sell some of the family land, he left Sam in charge. The interim subeditor literally took a page from big-city editors who stirred controversy with mock feuds and ad hominem attacks on their peers in order to attract readers, and he took a cue from Ben Franklin, who in 1722 contributed columns under a pseudonym to the *New-England Courant*, his brother James's newspaper. In "Blabbing Government Secrets" Sam invented the W. Epaminondas Adrastus Blab persona to criticize the Democratic governor of Missouri and its Democratic legislature for squandering time and tax money.[67]

But the more immediate target of his satire was J. T. Hinton, editor of the rival *Tri-Weekly Messenger*. Orion had recently complained about the noise of barking dogs in town, and Hinton had responded by branding Orion "a fierce hater of the canine race." During Orion's absence, Hinton was jilted and apparently resolved to drown himself in Bear Creek before changing his mind. The affair became grist for the local gossip mill. Hinton was "a simpering coxcomb of the first water," according to Sam, and posed as "an inveterate woman-killer," so the teenaged interim editor decided to ridicule him. He "wrote an elaborately wretched account of the whole matter" for the *Journal* "and then illustrated it" with a "villainous" woodcut engraved with a jackknife of Hinton with the head of a dog and "a lantern, sounding the depth of the water with a walking-stick. I thought it was desperately funny." Seeing it in print "was a joy which rather exceeded anything in that line I have ever experienced since," Sam declared sixty years later. The finger piece appeared in the September 16 issue of the paper and, Sam allowed, "I never knew any little thing to attract so much attention" as his "playful trifle. . . . For once the *Hannibal Journal* was in demand—a novelty it had not experienced before." Hinton was outraged, of course. He stormed the *Journal* office the next morning with a shotgun, Sam recalled, but when "he found that it was an infant (as he called me) that had done him the damage, he simply pulled my ears and went away." Whether or not he actually confronted Sam, Hinton replied to his insinuations in the next *Messenger*. His antagonist has neither "the decency of a gentleman, nor the honor of a blackguard," he charged, but "displays an amount of egotism that is a universal characteristic of all blackguards" and dismissed Sam's insults as "the feeble eminations [*sic*] of a puppy's brain."[68]

Orion "was very angry when he got back—unreasonably so," Sam thought, "considering what an impetus I had given the paper"—but "he softened," Sam claimed, "when he looked at the accounts and saw that I had actually booked the unparalleled number of thirty-three new subscribers, and had the vegetables to show for it, cordwood, cabbage, beans, and unsalable turnips enough to run the family for two years!" Orion allowed that the tempest in a teapot had "riveted the town's attention, but not its admiration." He tried to calm the waters in the next issue of the paper with a nonapology apology: "The jokes of our correspondent have been rather rough, but originating and perpetrated in a spirit of fun, and without a serious thought, no attention was expected to be paid to them, beyond a smile at the local editor's expense." In the same issue, Blab announced that he had "retired from public life to the shades of Glasscock's Island," three miles downstream from Hannibal.[69] Blab never again contributed to the columns of the *Journal*. Still, Sam remembered, "it took [his brother] several weeks to quiet down and pacify the people whom my writings had excited."[70]

The brouhaha did not prevent Orion from leaving Sam in charge again the following May when he went to St. Louis on business for ten days or so. Orion had launched a daily edition of the *Journal* in March and its condition was so fragile he may have admonished his younger brother to publish nothing that would cause a stir. If so, Sam ignored the admonition. On page 1 of the issue of the *Journal* for May 12, the day after his brother's departure, Sam inserted an ironic disclaimer with a sarcastic jab at his brother: "The Editor left yesterday for St. Louis. This must be our excuse if the paper is lacking in interest." The several issues of the *Hannibal Daily Journal* published in his absence again betray Sam's heavy editorial hand. He obviously wanted to spice up the pages of the paper. On the first day he printed a bit of his own tortured verse titled "Love Concealed" ("Oh, thou wilt never know how fond a love / This heart could have felt for thee"),[71] and the next day he editorially praised people with red hair, including Jesus and Thomas Jefferson (and by implication, his mother) in the mock-epic sketch "Oh, She Has a Red Head." With characteristic ingenuity he contended that the local whiskey tax made chugging liquor a civic duty, and he lambasted the Hannibal City Council for voting to ban Sunday liquor sales. As far back as February 1853,

Orion had begun to reprint articles from temperance journals in support of the local effort to suppress the liquor trade, but Sam neither shared his view nor approved it. As he explained, local residents would either buy liquor legally on Sunday, if available, or illegally from bootleggers, if necessary. In his opinion, the health risks to Hannibalians sickened by adulterated moonshine bought on Sunday trumped the calls to prohibit legal liquor sales on the Sabbath. Sam was outspoken on the issue: "Now we think that if this is the effect of stringent temperance laws; if the health, comfort and happiness of free people are to be obstructed, and their rights trampled upon in this manner, then I say, for one, that this is no longer a free country; and that our constitution is abused, and we had best not have any at all."[72]

Orion could not have been pleased that during his absence Sam had expressed a view in print contrary to his own editorial position. The best circumstantial evidence suggests that Sam and his brother had a spat soon after Orion's return from St. Louis in late May. Sam had filled the paper with his own poems, criticized his editorial policy on Sunday liquor sales, and fabricated a silly dispute between two fictional contributors, Rambler and Grumbler. Moreover, the seventeen-year-old Sam, who worked long hours for Orion for nothing more than room and board, wanted to buy a pistol, but his older brother refused to advance him the money. Orion tried to placate his brother by giving him the honorific title of editorial assistant and his own column in the paper—which lasted exactly three issues. In one of his columns, Sam lampooned Abner Gilstrap, editor of the Bloomington, Illinois, *Republican*. In the *Journal* for May 23, Sam made Gilstrap the target of a satirical parody of Charles Wolfe's poem "The Burial of Sir John Moore after Corunna." Cities across the region, including Bloomington, were quarreling over the route of the Hannibal and St. Joseph Railroad, so Sam picked a fight with Gilstrap, who thought his town—instead of Hannibal, by then the second-largest city in Missouri—should have been selected as the terminus of a major rail route west. "It struck me that it would make good, interesting matter to charge" Gilstrap "with a piece of gratuitous rascality" and watch him "squirm," Sam remembered.[73] Orion apparently had not seen the poem before it appeared in print, else he likely would have quashed it. He had always tried to conciliate rival editors, but Sam ridiculed them. In short, the crude parody hastened the inevitable.

Sam chafed under Orion's authority like Tom Sawyer sewn into his Sunday shirt, and in early June he quit the paper. Orion admitted later that he had been

> tyrannical and unjust to Sam. He was as swift and as clean as a good journeyman. I gave him tasks, and if he got through well I begrudged him the time

and made him work more. He set a clean proof, and Henry a very dirty one. The correcting was left to be done in the form the day before publication. Once we were kept late, and Sam complained with tears of bitterness that he was held till midnight on Henry's dirty proofs.

In his final "Assistant's Column" in the *Journal* for May 26, Sam noted that "from fifteen to twenty thousand persons are continually congregated around the new Crystal Palace in New York City, and drunkenness and debauching are carried on to their fullest extent." He was attracted to the spectacle like a moth to a flame. Frustrated and itching for a change, much as Franklin fled his apprenticeship in his brother's print shop rather than continue to submit to his authority, Sam "ran away" from home, as he put it, without so much as a fine howdy-do to Orion.[74]

CHAPTER 4

Journeyman Printer

I disappeared one night and fled to St. Louis. There I worked in the composing-room of the *Evening News* for a time, and then started on my travels to see the world.

—Autobiography of Mark Twain

In late may 1853 Sam Clemens left Hannibal and, according to his brother Orion, "went wandering in search of that comfort and that advancement and those rewards of industry which he had failed to find where I was—gloomy, taciturn, and selfish." Leaving aside the ambiguity of the statement—who, exactly, was "gloomy, taciturn, and selfish"?—the older brother admitted that he "not only missed" Sam's labor but that "we all missed his bounding activity and merriment." At his mother's insistence, Sam took an oath on the Bible not to throw a card or drink a drop of intoxicating liquor or swear during his journey. Jane Clemens claimed many years later that "that oath saved him." Sam caught the night boat for St. Louis on the initial leg of his first great adventure. Orion advertised for a new apprentice from May 27 until June 10. With the loss of Sam's assistance, Orion suspended publication of the *Daily Journal* for an entire month, from June 11 until July 11, even though the daily edition mostly consisted of boilerplate, and of both the daily and weekly editions of the paper on September 22. The *Hannibal Courier* published a satirical obituary to the effect that the paper had died of "a protracted and painful attack of *water on the brain*"—that is, as the result of Orion's advocacy of temperance—"and was consoled and tenderly cared for by a host of benevolent old ladies." By the end of the month Orion had folded his tent in Hannibal and sold the backlog of advertising in the *Journal* to William League of the *Whig Messenger* for five hundred dollars, the amount of his debt. He purchased a half interest in the *Muscatine Journal* and moved over two hundred miles north to the free state of Iowa with his mother and Henry. No member of the Clemens family ever lived in Hannibal again. The first issue of the *Muscatine Journal* under his co-ownership appeared on September 30.[1]

Meanwhile, Sam found work in the shop of the St. Louis *Evening News* and in the composing room of Thomas Ustick, Orion's former employer. With a population of about ninety thousand, including about two thousand slaves and about fifteen hundred free men and women of color, soon to become the eighth-largest metropolis in the nation, the Mound City at the time boasted twenty-one daily and weekly newspapers; twelve magazines; a half-dozen lithographic, printing, and engraving establishments; "four steel and copper plate engraving and three wood engraving" businesses; and "six book binderies and eight book and job offices." In all, these businesses employed over 850 printers—that is, about 1 percent of the population of the city worked in the printing industry. Ustick was responsible for producing the *Western Watchman*; the St. Louis *Presbyterian*; *Anzeiger des Westens*, an antislavery German-language daily; and other local publications. Sam no doubt learned some rudimentary German in Ustick's shop and, as soon as he was settled, began to save his money. He was a competent though not a skilled compositor, fully able to set around ten thousand ems during an eight-hour shift, but when he increased his speed to boost his income he multiplied his mistakes. "While the rest of us were drawing our $12 a week, it was all Sam Clemens could do to make $8 or $9," a coworker at the *Evening News* remembered. "He always had so many errors marked in his proofs that it took most of his time correcting them." Nor could he "have set up an advertisement in acceptable form to save his life." Sam likely lived with his sister Pamela and her husband Will on Pine Street to save the cost of renting a room. In a vain effort to make a little extra money, or so he recalled, he wrote several pieces he thought worthy of publication and carried them to the door of the editor of the St. Louis *Missouri Republican*, though he fled in trepidation before he submitted them for examination. While employed by the *Evening News*, he joined the St. Louis Typographical Union—his first but not last expression of solidarity with the cause of organized labor and craft guilds.[2]

As usual, he enjoyed an active social life. He dated a "shy pretty girl from up country," taking her to see *Toodles* at Ben de Bar's theater. In fact, he frequented the city theaters, befriending the Bateman sisters, Kate and Ellen, whose acting in such stage spectacles as *Aladdin or the Wonderful Lamp* at the St. Louis Theater attracted crowds of "charmed and worshiping admirers." At ages thirteen and eleven, Sam remembered, the sisters "were beautiful little creatures, and a delight to look upon." Fourteen years later, he alluded to the play and to his reading of the *Arabian Nights* to explain why he had not yet married: he was a poor scribbler and "I can't turn an inkstand into Aladdin's Lamp." By mid-August he had quit his jobs. Out of work, he "didn't fancy loafing in such a dry place as St. Louis," he informed his mother. Nonetheless, he assured her that he was keeping his promise to her to refrain from demon rum. "The most remarkable thing I remember about Clemens," his coworker recalled, "is the fact that he was not 'one of the boys.' Then, more than now, it was the proud prerogative of printers to be able to drink more red whiskey than men of any other trade. But Clemens, so far as I can remember, never took a drink."[3]

Jane Clemens believed Sam had merely moved to St. Louis to find work, but he wanted to see the world and by the world he meant New York. On August 19, 1853, he boarded the *Cornelia* for Alton, Illinois; took a train from Alton to Springfield; and then a stagecoach from Springfield to Bloomington. The next day he railed to Chicago; then passed through Toledo to Monroe, Michigan. On August 22 he sailed to Buffalo aboard a Lake Erie steamer and the next day he entrained from Buffalo, headed to Albany. As he passed through Rochester, he was reminded of the "rappings" of the Fox sisters in 1848, an early suggestion of his interest in spiritualism. In Syracuse he saw the courthouse where the fugitive slave Jerry McReynolds had been jailed "to prevent [his] rescue . . . by the infernal abolitionists." He finally arrived in New York aboard a Hudson River steamer early in the morning on August 24 with two or three dollars in his pocket and a ten-dollar bill sewn into the lining of his coat—or so he claimed later. He soon found work that paid about two dollars a day or ten dollars a week in the shop of John A. Gray & Green on Cliff Street, where two hundred men set in type such magazines as *Littell's Living Age*, the *Jewish Chronicle*, the New York *Recorder*, the *Choral Advocate*, and the *Knickerbocker*. "The price I get is 23 cents" per thousand ems, he wrote his mother, "but I did very well to get a place at all, for there are thirty or forty—yes, fifty good printers in the city with no work at all." He rented a room in a "sufficiently villainous mechanics' boarding house" on Duane Street on the Lower West Side, ten blocks from his workplace, that cost $3.50 a week. As in St. Louis, in his spare time he attended the theater, including productions of *Uncle Tom's Cabin* at Barnum's American Museum on Anne Street and Robert Montgomery Bird's *The Gladiator*, starring Edwin Forrest, at the Broadway Theater. *Uncle Tom's Cabin* "had already run one hundred and fifty nights" and its audiences attended "in elegant toilettes and cried over Tom's griefs," he groused. The role of Spartacus in Bird's play was, according to Forrest's official biographer, "the most 'physical' and 'melodramatic'" of all the parts in the actor's repertoire. Sam again joined the local typographical union, which entitled him to frequent a pair of libraries free to members and where he could "spend my evenings most pleasantly."[4] They were no doubt the Printers' Free Library and Reading Room on Chambers Street and the library of the General Society of Mechanics and Tradesmen at 32 Crosby Street, the second-oldest library in the city.[5] He was especially attracted by the Crystal Palace of the first World's Fair, near the Latting Observatory and the Croton Reservoir on Sixth Avenue between Fortieth and Forty-Second Streets, the site today of Bryant Park and the main building of the New York Public Library. He was impressed that a daily average of some six thousand visitors—twice the population of Hannibal—paid fifty cents apiece to enter the Palace. Moreover, from the top of the observatory, he wrote his sister Pamela, "you can obtain a grand view of the city and the country round." On the more exotic side, he attended to a "model artist show" or "leg show" at a theater on Chatham Street in lower Manhattan, probably Mademoiselle Couret's ensemble. It was a precursor of striptease, in which women in various stages of dishabille assumed poses of Greek statues. It was "horrid" and "immoral," and "everybody growled about it," and "people wouldn't go to see it," Sam remembered sixteen years later.[6] (Or, as Yogi Berra might have said, "Nobody goes there anymore. It's too crowded.") Eventually the police had to close it.

Sam was neither prepared nor willing to reconcile with Orion. To judge from extant letters, Sam only wrote his mother and sister for several months after his departure from Hannibal. He did not mention Orion in any of these letters until early September 1853, and he did not write his older brother until late October, four months after he left home. Nor did he adjust easily to the metropolis. He was disturbed by what he observed in New York, especially the race mixing and the "trundle-bed trash" he saw every morning as he walked to work through the Five Points. As he wrote Jane Clemens a week after his arrival in the city, "Niggers, mulattoes, quadroons, Chinese, and some the Lord no doubt originally intended to be white, but the dirt on whose faces leaves one uncertain as to that fact, block up the little, narrow street; and to wade through this mass of human vermin would raise the ire of the most patient person that ever lived."[7] In his response to the spectacle he betrayed his ingrained racism: "I reckon I had better black my face, for in these Eastern States niggers are considerably better than white people." From his perspective, the black folks he met in the East were insufficiently deferential. As he wrote, "I would like amazingly to see a good, old-fashioned negro." But by early October he admitted to Pamela that he had "taken a liking" to New York "and every time I get ready to leave, I put it off a day or so."[8]

His letters from New York also contain the earliest evidence of his morbid fascination with misshapen bodies and human deformity. He wrote his mother that he had seen the so-called Wild Men of Borneo, a pair of sideshow freaks exhibited by P. T. Barnum at his dime museum: "Two beings, about like common people, with the exception of their faces, which are more like the 'phiz' of an orang-outang, than human. . . . [They] are supposed to be a cross between man and orang-outang; one is the best natured being in the world, while the other would tear a stranger to pieces, if he did but touch him. . . . Their faces and eyes are those of the beast." For the rest of his life, Sam was intrigued by such "human curiosities." Returning to Barnum's Dime Museum in New York in March 1867 he observed "two dwarfs, unknown to fame, and a speckled Negro." After touring the U.S. Capitol in late 1867 he remarked in his journal on Thaddeus Stevens's clubfoot. He based his comic sketches "Two-Headed Girls" (1869) and "Personal Habits of the Siamese Twins" (1869), his introduction of his friends Bill Nye and James Whitcomb Riley at Tremont Temple in Boston in 1889, and his novella *Those Extraordinary Twins* (1894) on the experience of conjoined twins. (One of them was a Catholic and the other a Baptist, one a drunk and the other a teetotaler, one fought for the Confederacy and the other for the Union, they were two years apart in age, one swallowed food the other digested, one slept while the other snored, etc.) In Jim Blaine's story of his grandfather's old ram in *Roughing It* (1872), "old Miss Wagner" borrows both a glass eye and a wooden leg from "old Miss Jefferson." Traces of Sam's macabre fascination with physical grotesqueries also appear in "The Facts Concerning the Recent Carnival of Crime in Connecticut" (1876), in which the narrator's conscience haunts him in the guise of "a shriveled, shabby" anthropomorphized dwarf, a "vile bit of human rubbish," who is "covered all over with a fuzzy, greenish mold, such as one sometimes sees upon mildewed bread"; *Adventures of Huckleberry Finn* (1885), in which Joanna Wilks has a "hare-lip," or cleft palate; and *Personal Recollections of Joan of Arc* (1896), in which the eponymous heroine pardons a seven-foot giant ironically nicknamed the Dwarf. Sam reminisced as late as February 1906 about "a lonely and melancholy little hunchback" who had run a Hannibal cigar store.[9]

In an effort to improve his situation, he finally resigned his position with Gray & Green and traveled to Philadelphia, the second-largest city in the country, via the Camden and Amboy Railroad around October 20, 1853. He shared a room in a boardinghouse with an Englishman named Sumner and within a week he was working the graveyard shift as a substitute printer for the *Philadelphia Inquirer*, the largest morning local. "I go to work at 7 o'clock in the evening, and work till 3 o'clock the next morning," he wrote Orion. "I can go to the theatre and stay till 12 o'clock and then go to the office, and get work from that till 3 the next morning; when I go to bed, and sleep till 11 o'clock, then get up and loaf the rest of the day." He initially bragged that he was easily able to earn $2.50 per shift, setting ten to eleven thousand ems in type. Still, he "was laughed at by all the hands" in the shop, "the poorest of whom sets 11,000 on Sunday." Of the twenty-two compositors with whom

he worked, at least twelve "set 15,000 on Sunday." A month later, he conceded that for some reason he could not "set type nearly so fast as when I was at
home. Sunday is a long day, and while others set 12 and 15,000, yesterday, I
only set 10,000."[10]

Meanwhile, he played the tourist and sent Orion a pair of letters for
publication in the *Muscatine Journal*. In them Sam described his visits to
the graves of Benjamin and Deborah Franklin in Germantown; Carpenter's Hall, where the first U.S. Congress assembled; the campus of Gi-
rard College; and the original Fairmont Park. On the "sacred ground" of
Independence Hall, where the declaration was signed, he experienced "an
unaccountable feeling of awe and reverence." He reclined on a pine bench
where Franklin and George Washington had once sat and, in a letter to his
mother and sister, admitted that he had repressed the temptation to whittle
off a chip. He crisscrossed the city by horsecar, citing without credit R. A.
Smith's *Philadelphia as It Is in 1852* in his correspondence with the *Journal*.
Sam's tendency to paraphrase or plagiarize from guidebooks eventually became almost routine, especially in his travel writings. He may have acquired
the habit—and thought nothing of it—while copying from newspaper exchanges at the typecase.

Smith	Sam
Philadelphia is, perhaps, the most healthy city in the U.S. The air is sweet and clear.	Philadelphia is one of the healthiest places in the Union. The air is pure and fresh.
In the year 1681, the first settlers arrive from London, in the ship "Sarah and John," Captain Smith.	It was about 1682 that this city was laid out. The first settlers came over the year previously, in the "Sarah and John," Capt. Smith.
The State House, or Independence Hall.—This Interesting Relic of the past deserves special notice, and few strangers leave our city without visiting its venerated halls. . . . The original cost was £5,600.	The old State House in Chestnut Street, is an object of great interest to the stranger, and though it has often been repaired, the old model and appearance are still preserved. It is a substantial edifice, and its original cost was £5,600.
Carpenter's Hall.—This edifice is situated in Carpenter's Court. . . . This celebrated building will be cherished by the friends of American Independence. Within its walls the first Congress . . . assembled.	Carpenter's Hall, situated in Carpenter's Court, is a pile dear to every American, for within its walls, the first Congress of the United States assembled.[11]

In the first flush of his pleasure in Philadelphia, Sam admitted to his sister that it had been "as hard on my conscience to leave New York, as it was easy to leave Hannibal." But he soon adjusted to the rhythms of the Quaker City. "Unlike New York, I like this Phila[delphia] amazingly," he wrote on October 26. But succumbing to the xenophobia common at the time, he was put off by the number of "abominable foreigners" he encountered. He complained when he visited the shop of the Philadelphia *North American* that "there was at least one foreigner [*sic*] for every American at work there." He was particularly offended by the Irish immigrants who worked beside him at the *Inquirer* and "hate everything American." He had never seen before "so many whisky-swilling, God-despising heathens as I find in this part of the country. I believe I am the only person in the *Inquirer* office that does not drink." He was still honoring his oath to his mother. He soon adapted to the local custom, however, including what the printers called "a 'free-and-easy' at the saloons" on Saturday nights, when "a chairman is appointed, who calls on any of the assembled company for a song or recitation." As he wrote home, "It is hard to get tired of Philadelphia, for amusements are not scarce."[12]

Still, he was scarcely able to earn more than a subsistence and he complained that the "incessant night-work" in the print shops was damaging his eyes and dulling his mind. He tarried in Philadelphia until mid-February 1854, when he took a brief furlough over a long weekend to Washington, D.C., on what he called "a flying trip . . . to see the sights." He did not apparently look for work, though he wrote an account of the trip for the *Muscatine Journal*. The city as a whole he thought "a wide stretch of cheap little brick houses, with here and there a noble architectural pile lifting itself out of the midst—government buildings, these." He attended a performance of *Othello* starring Edwin Forrest at the National Theater on the evening of February 17—in the first flush of his fame, Forrest had only recently added the role to his repertoire. The Treasury building, he thought, "would command respect in any capital" and the redbrick Smithsonian Institution seemed "half-church and half-castle." The White House reminded him of "a fine large white barn, with wide unhandsome grounds about it. . . . It is ugly enough outside, but that is nothing to what it is inside. Dreariness, flimsiness, bad taste reduced to mathematical completeness is what the inside offers to the eye." He was more impressed by Clark Mills's statue of Andrew Jackson commemorating the Battle of New Orleans, recently unveiled in Lafayette Square, across Pennsylvania Avenue from the Executive Mansion. Construction on the Washington Monument, begun in 1848, had stalled at only about 150 feet, a mere stub of what had been planned and less than a third of its final height of 555 feet, because its private funding had been exhausted. Still, Sam thought it towered "out of the mud—sacred soil is the customary term. It has the aspect of a factory chimney with the top broken off. The skeleton of a decaying scaffolding lingers about its summit, and tradition says that the spirit of Washington often comes down and sits on those rafters to enjoy this tribute of respect which the nation has reared as the symbol of its unappeasable gratitude." The obelisk would finally be completed in 1888. Sam was particularly impressed by the Museum of the Patent Office, with its exhibit of ancient Peruvian mummies, Washington's military uniform, the original Declaration of Independence, and a printing press that Franklin had owned in London. In chapter 28 of *The Innocents Abroad* (1869) he compared piety and pragmatism, what Henry Adams would call "the virgin and the dynamo" over a half century later. If the Vatican contained "all that is curious and beautiful in art," he opined, then "in our Patent Office is hoarded all that is curious or useful in mechanics." In *A Connecticut Yankee in King Arthur's Court* (1889), moreover, Hank Morgan, aka "the Boss," establishes a patent office on the first day of his administration because "I knew that a country without a patent office and good patent laws was just a crab, and couldn't travel any way but sideways or backwards."

But the U.S. Capitol was the public building that most impressed Sam. Standing on "the verge of a high piece of table land, a fine commanding position," with its white marble facade and "great rotunda," the "temple of liberty" was, he thought, "a very noble and a very beautiful building, both within and without." During his visit to the public galleries there he watched as the Senate and the House of Representatives debated the Kansas-Nebraska Act and the repeal of the Missouri Compromise. On the Senate side he heard speeches by Lewis Cass of Michigan, Stephen A. Douglas of Illinois, and William Seward of New York. Seward struck him as "a slim, dark, bony individual" who looked "like a respectable wind would blow him out of the country." On the House side he observed Thomas Hart Benton, the former senator from Missouri, sitting "silent and gloomy in the midst of the din, like a lion imprisoned in a cage of monkeys, who, feeling his superiority, disdains to notice their chattering." As in New York, Sam complained about the racial diversity of the city, comparing Washington to "a Hottentot village." According to the 1850 census, nearly one-third of the more than fifty thousand residents of the District of Columbia were black, over ten thousand of them free men and women of color. A decade before the abolition of slavery in the district in 1862—and well before the Great Migration from the South of the early twentieth century—it had become a destination for free blacks.[13]

After four days Sam returned to Philadelphia, where during the spring and summer of 1854 he set type for the Philadelphia *Public Ledger* and

Philadelphia *North American*. One of the conventions of the former paper, he explained in 1870, was to append to death notices "a verse or two of comforting poetry. . . . There is an element about some poetry which is able to make even physical suffering and death cheerful things to contemplate and consummation to be desired. This element is present in the mortuary poetry of Philadelphia." The death of a child was just as "surely followed by a burial" as "by the accustomed solacing poesy in the 'Public Ledger.'" Sam admitted to Albert Bigelow Paine over sixty years later that he had "offered his contributions to the Philadelphia *Ledger*—mainly poetry of the obituary kind," though his submissions had been refused. He was reticent to discuss the matter even in his anecdotage. "All he ever said" of the episode, according to Paine, was that "my efforts were not received with approval." But at least one of his obituary poems, titled "The Swiss Girl's Home" and signed "S.L.C.," reached print in the *Portland Transcript*, a Maine literary weekly and one of the *Public Ledger*'s exchanges, for May 24, 1854:

> A Swiss girl lay on her dying bed,
>   Far from her native land,
> And wildly thought in troubled dreams
>   By childhood's home to stand.
> With fancy's eye, she saw the cot,
>   And shadowy mountains round,
> And heard the Swiss boy's ringing horn
>   Far through the valley sound.
> But all was changed, for they were gone,
>   Who gave the scene its charm,
> The grey-haired father's stooping form,
>   Her mother's brow so calm.
> With aching heart, she turned away,
>   "This is no home for me"—
> She started up with heavenly joy,
>   "Oh what is this I see?"
> "I see a city built of gold,
>   With pearly gates so fair,
> No sun doth shine, or day doth dawn,
>   Nor sorrow enter there."
> "Before God's throne, bright angels throng,
>   My Father's face I see,
> A blessed home I've found at last,
>   Dear ones I come to thee."

Strange as it may seem, this doggerel—with its archaic diction, lockstep meter, and maudlin sentimentality—betrays all the earmarks of the hackneyed verse Sam had written earlier for the *Hannibal Journal*. And it resembles in particular "The Heart's Lament," the utterly conventional ode composed in twenty-four lines of iambic tetrameter that had appeared in the *Daily Journal* the previous year. "The Swiss Girl's Home" also shares a rhyme and metrical scheme with Felicia Hemans's chestnut "Casabianca," and it foreshadows a dream Becky Thatcher has while she and Tom are lost in McDougal's Cave in *Tom Sawyer*: "I've seen such a beautiful country in my dream," Becky tells Tom. "I reckon we are going there."[14] That is, at age eighteen Sam was fully able to compose with a straight face the type of stricken verse he burlesqued in Emmeline Grangerford's "Ode to Stephen Dowling Bots, Dec'd" in chapter 17 of *Huck Finn*.

Sam returned briefly to New York from Philadelphia—no details survive of this trip—before he beat a hasty retreat to Muscatine. In December 1853 a fire in the New York print shops of Harper & Bros. and George F. Colledge & Bros., while he was working in Philadelphia, had thrown dozens of typesetters out of work in an already depressed job market. Sam reluctantly surrendered to the financial stress of trying to survive on a jour printer's income at the end of his Wanderjahr, as he explained in 1899. He traveled sometime in late spring or early summer 1854 back to St. Louis, "sitting upright in the smoking-car two or three days and nights," then connecting by steamboat to Muscatine. He was so tired he "fell asleep at once, with my clothes on, and didn't wake again for thirty-six hours." Throughout the trip, some twelve hundred miles without a layover, Sam's "head was in a turmoil night and day fierce enough and exhausting enough to upset a stronger reason than mine." For protection he traveled with a revolver he had purchased in the East, though he remarked in jest when he finally arrived at Orion's home that he had bought it to kill his brother. That is, he returned home with a pistol in his pocket if only to prove he no longer needed his brother's permission to pack it.[15]

But Sam had no future in Muscatine. For that matter, neither did Orion. He was half owner of a Whig newspaper, but as soon as he settled there, he had changed his party affiliation from Whig to Republican to signal his opposition to the Kansas-Nebraska Act.[16] The act effectively repealed the Missouri Compromise and opened the western territories to "popular sovereignty"—that is, to settlement by slaveholders. Opponents of slavery, including Orion, were outraged, and passage of the act led inexorably to border ruffians like William Quantrill and to the rehearsal for the Civil War in "bloody Kansas."

Sam worked in the *Muscatine Journal* shop for a few weeks to earn a grub-stake. His most vivid memory of this period was of a lunatic named Bill Israeel, who

> caught me out in the fields, one Sunday, and extracted a butcher-knife from his boot and proposed to carve me up with it, unless I acknowledged him to be the only son of the Devil. I tried to compromise on an acknowledgment that he was the only member of the family I had met; but that did not satisfy him; he wouldn't have any half-measures; I must say he was the sole and only son of the Devil—he whetted his knife on his boot. It did not seem worthwhile to make trouble about a little thing like that; so I swung round to his view of the matter and saved my skin whole.[17]

He re-created the incident in chapters 20–21 of *The Prince and the Pauper* (1882), where a crazed hermit and self-described archangel (apparently a fallen one) threatens to kill young King Edward with a rusty butcher knife he slowly whets.

Sam returned to St. Louis by early August 1854, when he joined a citizen militia charged with suppressing a nativist riot. Thomas Hart Benton, standing (but defeated) for reelection to Congress, had appealed for immigrant votes and on election day, August 7, the local Know-Nothing firebrands in response marauded through the ethnic neighborhoods of the city, killing ten people, wounding thirty-three, and damaging nearly a hundred buildings. Sam likely sympathized more with the mob than with the militia he had joined. As Louis J. Budd notes, "it is fair to say that he watched" the riots "without disapproval." Nevertheless, from the window of his boardinghouse he "saw some of the fightings and killings" and so the next day he went "to an armory where two hundred young men had met, upon call, to be armed and go forth against the rioters, under command of a military man. We drilled till about ten o'clock at night; then news came that the mob were in great force in the lower end of the town, and were sweeping everything before them." The militia had been mobilized to protect the offices of *Anzeiger des Westens*, the German-language newspaper he had helped to typeset the year before, at Third Street between Chestnut and Market—a site that is today almost directly beneath the Gateway Arch. "Our column moved at once," Sam remembered. "It was a very hot night, and my musket was very heavy. We marched and marched; and the nearer we approached the seat of war, the hotter I grew and the thirstier I got. I was behind my friend; so, finally, I asked him to hold my musket while I dropped out and got a drink. Then I branched off and went home." Ironically, Sam soon remarked in one of his letters to the *Muscatine Journal* that police were "queer animals and have remarkably nice notions as to the great law of self-preservation. I doubt if the man is now living that ever caught one at a riot."[18] Not only does this comment anticipate Sam's lifelong criticism of police corruption and incompetence, but the incident also foreshadows Sam's "campaign that failed" seven years later, even to his desertion from the Marion Rangers at the outset of the Civil War. He always preferred flight to fight.

In St. Louis during these months Sam made an initial effort to become a riverboat pilot. "When I was a boy," he reminisced in "Old Times on the Mississippi" (1875), there was "but one permanent ambition among my comrades" in Hannibal. It was "to be a steamboatman. We had transient ambitions of other sorts, but they were only transient." He was so eager to go on the river that, at the age of sixteen, he persuaded a sailor to tattoo "an anchor and rope on the back of my left hand with India ink. The color was a deep, dark blue, and extravagantly conspicuous."[19] Sam approached the crews of a few boats "that lay packed together like sardines at the long St. Louis wharf" but "got only a cold shoulder and short words from mates and clerks." With a letter of introduction from Orion, he also approached James J. Clemens Jr. in August 1855 for a loan to pay a pilot to teach him the river, but his cousin refused. He had already advanced his poor relations plenty of money over the years, and he thought Sam "should stick to his present trade or art" rather than pursue a pipe dream.[20]

Sam resided in a boardinghouse at the corner of Fourth Avenue and Washington Street owned by the Pavey family, relatives of Hannibalians. "It was a large, cheap place & had in it a good many young fellows who were students at a Commercial College," he remembered. His roommate, Jacob Burrough, was a journeyman chairmaker, a rabid republican and autodidact "fond of Dickens, Thackeray, Scott & Disraeli" and the model for the character of Barrow in *The American Claimant* (1892), "a short man about forty years old, with sandy hair, no beard, and a pleasant face badly freckled but alive and intelligent, and he wore slop-shop clothing which was neat but showed wear." Sam and Burrough seem to have bonded over books. Sam remembered that his roommate was the only other lover of literature in the house. Twenty-two years later Sam conceded that at the time he had been "a callow fool, a self-sufficient ass, a mere human tumble-bug, stern in air, heaving at his bit of dung, imagining that he is remodeling the world and is entirely capable of doing it right. . . . Ignorance, intolerance, egotism, self-assertion, opaque perception, dense & pitiful chuckle-headedness—& an almost pathetic unconsciousness of it all. That is what I was at 19–20." Sam again became a habitué of the theater, attending performances of the St. Louis Varieties, *Ingomar the Barbarian* starring George W. Jamieson at the

People's Theater, and *The Merchant of Venice* ("I had always thought that this was a comedy, until they made a *farce* out of it").[21]

He returned to work for the *Evening News*, though he lasted there only a few months. "He was a good printer," his coworker William Waite remembered, "but mighty independent." After all, he had earned a living at his craft in busier shops and bigger cities. But he was occasionally tardy for work and Charles G. Ramsey, owner and editor of the *News*, badgered him. According to Waite, Ramsey "would say: 'Here's that —— boy late again,'" the type of rebuke Sam resented his whole life. "One morning he turned on Ramsey and replied: 'Take your dashed situation, and go to (a warm country)!'"— or words to that effect. "He left the office and we heard nothing of him for several years." After burning his bridges in St. Louis, Sam again fled upriver to rejoin Orion, who had recently resettled in Keokuk, Iowa.[22]

As Sam relates the tale in his autobiography, Orion was a victim of romantic entanglements when he became engaged to two women simultaneously, one of them Mollie Stotts of Keokuk, the daughter of one of his mother's friends, and the other "a winning and pretty girl" who lived forty miles away in Quincy, Illinois. "He didn't know whether to marry the Keokuk one or the Quincy one," Sam recalled in 1906, "or whether to try to marry both of them and suit everyone concerned. But the Keokuk girl soon settled that for him. She was a master spirit and she ordered him to write the Quincy girl and break off that match, which he did. Then he married the Keokuk girl and they began a struggle for life which turned out to be a difficult enterprise, and very unpromising." On December 19, 1854, Mollie and Orion were wed in Keokuk. On March 14, 1855, apparently at her insistence, Orion began to offer his half interest in the *Muscatine Journal* for sale; and in June 1855 they moved to Keokuk, population 650, eighty miles downriver from Muscatine, fifteen miles from Hannibal, and about two hundred miles north of St. Louis, so that she could be near her family.[23]

At the tender age of twenty, Mollie was nine years younger than Orion and a year older than Sam. But the way the younger brother told the story a quarter century later, she was a regular harridan and

> a bald-headed old maid. She was poor & taboo; she wanted position & clothes, oh, so badly; she had the snaffle on his ass before he knew what he was about—for he was editor of a daily paper & a good catch. She is saturated to the marrow with the most malignant form of Presbyterianism,—that sort which considers the saving of one's own paltry soul the first & supreme end & object of life. So you see she has harried him into the church several times, & then made religion so intolerable to him with her prayings & Bible readings

& her other & eternal pious clack-clack that it has had the effect of harrying him out of it again.

Orion "bought a little bit of a job-printing plant—on credit, of course—and at once put prices down to where not even the apprentices could get a living out of it."[24] After Orion married, Jane moved from Muscatine to St. Louis to live with the Moffetts.

On the surface, Orion's future again seemed promising. The proprietor of a print shop, unlike the editor of a newspaper, need not pander to public opinion, express political views, or hew a party line. When Sam arrived in Keokuk from St. Louis after quitting the *Evening News*, his brother offered him five dollars a week and board to work for him and Sam agreed. After all, he had no job in St. Louis to which he might return. "I worked in that little job office," he remembered, "without ever collecting a cent of wages, for Orion was never able to pay anything." Henry and Sam lived in the Ben Franklin Book and Job Office on the third floor of the Ogden Building on Main Street, much to the annoyance of the music teacher on the second floor, until Sam took singing and piano lessons from him. The range of Sam's musical talent was not extensive; according to his friend George F. Carvell, a fellow steamboatman, he could play but one song on the guitar, "Star of the Evening, Beautiful Star," and he sang and played on the piano only a handful of tunes, including a few Negro spirituals and "Grasshopper on the Sweet Potato Vine," a ditty about a horse by the name of Methusalem. But he continued to read widely. According to Paine, the residents of Keokuk remembered that Sam often carried around a volume of Edgar Allan Poe's tales. Several years later, Sam would publish a parody of Poe's "The Raven" in the Virginia City, Nevada, *Territorial Enterprise*.[25]

Coincidentally, the Keokuk real estate market began to boom in 1856, soon after Sam settled there. "Anything in the semblance of a town lot, no matter how situated, was salable," he recalled, "and at a figure which would still have been high if the ground had been sodded with greenbacks." The town grew like a mushroom in manure sheltered from the sun. According to the 1856 Keokuk directory, which Sam helped set in type, the city boasted twenty-three brickyards, the same number of lawyers, nineteen stone quarries, twelve churches, ten butcher shops, eight lumberyards, three breweries, and an undertaker. From only 620 residents in 1847 the population burgeoned to over 6,000 in 1855, when Sam moved there, to 11,000 a year later, and to 15,000 in 1857, the year he left. Over six hundred houses were erected in the town in 1856 alone. Sam bought several building lots in Keokuk at the height of the excitement, probably on credit. The next year property values plummeted, an early example of the poor investment decisions that plagued Sam his entire life. As Kevin Mac Donnell notes, "A downtown hotel was auctioned off in 1857 for unpaid taxes for one-tenth of what it had sold for the year before, and a thousand city lots were put up at public auction for back taxes. Lots that sold for $1,000 a few years before were sold for $10 in 1857." Keokuk "was one of the most stirring and enterprising young cities in America," Sam remembered a decade later, "but railroads and land speculations killed it in a single night, almost."[26] He resided in Keokuk for fifteen months and left just before the real estate crash, though he may have first worked briefly as a printer across the river in Warsaw, Illinois. It is among the least documented periods in his life and one of the few lacunae in the record.

While living in Keokuk, Sam became a temporary convert to phrenology, a pseudoscience that presumed a person's traits or "temperaments" could be judged by the curvature of the head. The belief anticipated his mature conviction that character is predetermined, a product of nature and nurture over which the individual has virtually no control. "One of the most frequent arrivals in our village of Hannibal was the peripatetic phrenologist," he remembered in his autobiography, "and he was popular, and always welcome. He gathered the people together and gave them a gratis lecture on the marvels of phrenology, then felt their bumps and made an estimate of the result, at twenty-five cents per head." When his own bumps were "read" or palpitated, Sam was told he possessed a well-developed organ of sanguinity. On the other hand, Orion—according to the lumps on his skull—possessed an overdeveloped "nervous temperament." Sam was so intrigued that he copied passages into his notebook almost verbatim from George Sumner Weaver's *Lectures on Mental Science According to the Philosophy of Phrenology* (1852). Though he later qualified his belief in the pseudoscience, even referring to "phrenological frauds" in *Tom Sawyer* and to phrenology as a "quack" branch of medicine in *Huck Finn*, he occasionally invoked its jargon for the rest of his life, as in a February 1862 letter to his mother and sister in which he cautioned them to avoid people with "the organ of Hope preposterously developed" and in chapter 31 of *Roughing It*, where he referred to a stage driver's "bump of locality."[27]

At the age of twenty, a handsome and eligible beau, Sam was romantically linked with "a right smart chance of gals in Keokuk," as he later put it. Among them were Ella Creel, his second cousin on the Lampton side of the family; Ella Patterson, a relative of his sister-in-law Mollie Clemens; Belle Stotts, Mollie's sister; Ann Virginia Ruffner, a visitor to Keokuk in May 1856 whom he escorted to church; Iowa Burns, who lived a block from the print shop; and the three daughters of a local alderman, near neighbors of

Mollie's family, Mary Jane (aka Mane), Esther (aka Ete), and especially their sister Annie Taylor. Both Mane and Annie were students at Iowa Wesleyan College in Mt. Pleasant, Iowa. Sam and Annie corresponded until at least June 1, 1857, and she subsequently became an English teacher at Lindenwood College in St. Charles, Missouri. Years later, Sam crossed paths with Mary Jane Taylor in the West. She died in Dayton, Nevada, in early September 1863 at the age of thirty-one.[28]

Sam delivered his first public speech on January 17, 1856, at a printers' banquet at the Ivins House, the best hotel in Keokuk, to celebrate the sesquicentennial of the birth of Benjamin Franklin. Unfortunately, no transcript of the address survives, though Orion described it in the next issue of the Keokuk *Gate City* as "replete with wit and humor," adding that it had been "interrupted by long and continuous bursts of applause." One of Sam's coworkers also remembered the occasion: "Blushing and slowly getting upon his feet, stammering in the start, he finally rallied his powers, and when he sat down, his speech was pronounced by all present a remarkable production of pathos and wit, the latter, however, predominating, convulsing his hearers with round after round of applause." Sam was soon recruited to join a local debating society. Meanwhile, the printing of the city directory that he supervised, issued in June 1856, "did not pay largely," according to Paine, because Orion "was always too eager for the work; too low in his bid for it." Sam listed his own occupation in it as an "antiquarian." The term is significant because, in one of his columns in the *Hannibal Journal* in May 1853, he had mentioned the recent discovery of "ruins of ancient cities" in Mexico—no doubt the allegedly lost Aztec city of Iximaya—that was the subject of Pedro Velasquez's fanciful *Memoir of an Eventful Expedition in Central America* (published in English in 1850). He added that the news would interest an "antiquarian," his word for a type of explorer or anthropologist.[29]

Predictably, then, when Sam came across a copy of William Herndon's *Exploration of the Valley of the Amazon* (1854) in Keokuk, he was excited and intrigued. A passage about coca, an unregulated drug sometimes used in patent medicines, galvanized his interest. In particular, Herndon related a story about a native who

> worked hard for five nights and days without intermission, except for two hours each night—and this without food. Immediately after the work the Indian accompanied him on a two-day journey of twenty-three leagues on foot, and then declared that he was ready to engage in the same amount of work, and go through it without food, if he were allowed an abundance of coca. This man was sixty-two years of age, and had never been sick in his life.

According to Herndon, coca was "a powerful stimulant to the nervous system, and, like strong coffee or tea, to take away sleep; but, unlike tobacco and other stimulants, no one has known it to be injurious to the health." To Sam it seemed a "marvelous herb" without any negative side effects, so he decided to emigrate to Brazil and become a coca farmer. "I was fired with a longing to ascend the Amazon" and "to open up a trade in coca with all the world," he remembered. He nursed an ambition to explore the headwaters of the Amazon—or, more accurately, to exploit the narcotic effects of the coca plant for profit.[30] He conspired in the scheme with a pair of potential partners, one of them Joseph S. Martin, a local Keokuk doctor and faculty member at Iowa Medical College. He also tried to entice his nineteen-year-old brother Henry to join the expedition, but Henry first asked his mother's permission and approval. "If I have an opportunity to go, I am afraid it will not be easy to obtain Ma's consent," he advised Sam, and then he offered his own scrap of advice: "You seem to think Keokuk property is so good to speculate in, you'd better invest all your spare change in it, instead of going to South America." In the end, Sam left Keokuk alone.[31]

He embarked on his quixotic journey sometime before mid-October 1856. Later, in a characteristic embroidery of the facts, he claimed that he discovered a fifty-dollar banknote blowing in the wind that financed his excursion—"I advertised the find and left for the Amazon the same day," lest the owner claim the note—but no evidence corroborates this story.[32] Instead, Sam seems to have agreed to contribute a series of essays to the Keokuk *Saturday Post* for which he would be paid five dollars apiece. They were the first articles for which he was ever compensated. He boated south to St. Louis and, on October 13, he walked through the St. Louis Agricultural and Mechanical Association Fair and wrote up his observations of the "happily spent day" for the paper. Three of the next four pieces he sent the *Saturday Post* were published under the Dickensian pseudonym "Thomas Jefferson Snodgrass"—the nom de plume may allude to Jefferson's auburn hair, the same color as Sam's. Thomas Rees, son of George Rees, editor of the *Saturday Post*, boasted years later that his father had "discovered" Mark Twain. According to the son, "The firm of Rees & Son arranged with the young man to write some articles for publication in the *Keokuk Post*, which they mutually agreed would be worth five dollars each." After submitting one or two from St. Louis, Sam demanded an increase in pay and Rees met his demand. He then submitted three more columns from Cincinnati and upped the ante by demanding ten or fifteen dollars for any additional columns. George Rees refused to meet his price and, as Thomas Rees put it, "the series of articles ended at that point." Sam had overpriced his wares. It was his first clash with a publisher, but hardly his last. In his autobiographical dictation, Sam protested his innocence: "Did I write the rubbish with which Mr. Rees charges me? I suppose not. I have no reason to suppose that I wrote it, but I can't say, and I don't say that I didn't write it." He never denied categorically that he was the author of the Snodgrass letters, however, and he elsewhere reported that early in his career he had contributed to the *Saturday Evening Post*, an apparent misremembering of the Keokuk *Saturday Post*.[33]

The Snodgrass letters are written in the voice of an unsophisticated rube, a backwoods bumpkin, a distant and intellectually stunted cousin of Huck Finn. The first of the three letters, written on October 18 after Sam attended a performance of *Julius Caesar* in St. Louis, burlesques Shakespeare. Snodgrass belonged to the cacographical "school of bad spelling" and dialect humor founded by such regional literary comedians as Artemus Ward, Petroleum V. Nasby, and Josh Billings. Much of this comedy consists of mangled syntax and eye dialect (e.g., "dierrea" for "diary," "Cashus" for "Cassius," "wimmim" for "women," "laffin" for "laughing," etc.), a convention of Southwestern humor that Sam rarely (ab)used in the years to come. The second Snodgrass letter recounts his "voyage" from St. Louis to Cincinnati. Rather than rail directly from St. Louis to Cincinnati or catch a steamboat downstream to Cairo and up the Ohio River, however, Snodgrass (that is, Sam) took a much more circuitous route—from St. Louis to Keokuk in mid-October to see Rees and negotiate payment for the Snodgrass letters, back downstream to Quincy, then by rail to Chicago and Indianapolis, finally arriving in Cincinnati about October 24. He found work in the print shop of T. Wrightson & Co. on Walnut Street and a room in a boardinghouse three blocks away on Third Street. With five daily and fifteen weekly newspapers and a population of about 150,000, the Queen City was a publishing center for the western United States, with a lucrative job market for printers. Ironically, twenty-year-old W. D. Howells worked for a time a block away from Sam, though the two men would not meet formally for thirteen more years. Sam's fellow boarders were, he remembered, "commonplace people of various ages and both sexes. They were full of bustle, frivolity, chatter and the joy of life and were good-natured, clean-minded and well-meaning; but they were oppressively uninteresting, for all that—with one exception."[34]

He soon befriended the exception, a Scot whom he later called Macfarlane—in fact, probably John J. McFarland, who was not only Sam's fellow boarder but his coworker at Wrightson & Co. Macfarlane was a "diligent talker" about "forty years old—just double my age—but we were opposites in most ways and comrades from the start." The winter of 1856–57, Sam reported in his third Snodgrass letter, was one of the harshest on record. (The coldest winter he ever spent was a winter in Cincinnati?) First the snow fell "tell you actilly couldn't see the mud in the streets," Snodgrass reported. "Next it kivered up and blotted out the sines, and continued on tell all the brick houses looked like the frame ones, and visy versy," and eventually the "Ohio river was friz to the bottom." Sam spent his evenings "by the wood fire in [Macfarlane's] room, listening in comfort to his tireless talk and to the dulled complainings of the winter storms until the clock struck ten." While Macfarlane "had no humor, nor any comprehension of it," he owned "two or three dozen weighty books—philosophies, histories, and scientific works." Like Sam's friend Jacob Burrough in St. Louis, Macfarlane was an autodidact and religious skeptic, and he espoused a primitive evolutionary theory:

> Macfarlane considered that the animal life in the world was developed in the course of aeons of time from a few microscopic seed germs, or perhaps one microscopic seed germ deposited upon the globe by the Creator in the dawn of time, and that this development was progressive upon an ascending scale toward ultimate perfection until man was reached; and that then the progressive scheme broke pitifully down and went to wreck and ruin! He said that man's heart was the only bad heart in the animal kingdom; that man was the only animal capable of feeling malice, envy, vindictiveness, revengefulness, hatred, selfishness, the only animal that loved drunkenness, almost the only animal that could endure personal uncleanliness and a filthy habitation, the sole animal in whom was fully developed the base instinct called patriotism, the sole animal that robs, persecutes, oppresses, and kills members of his own immediate tribe, the sole animal that steals and enslaves the members of any *tribe*.[35]

Whether or not Sam accurately characterizes Macfarlane's theory, he remembered it in a way that clearly resonated with his own subsequent reading of Charles Darwin and Alfred Russel Wallace and his convictions late in life about the "damned human race."

Sam paid a sixteen-dollar fare and on February 16, 1857, he finally left Cincinnati aboard the *Paul Jones*, a 353-ton side-wheeler traveling from Pittsburgh to New Orleans. From there he planned to embark on the next ship sailing for Para, Brazil, and the Amazon. He described the steamboat in "Old Times on the Mississippi" as an "ancient tub," and, following his lead, Paine described it as an "ancient little craft" and Samuel Charles Webster mocked it as the "ramshackle *Paul Jones*." But Sam's description of the ship was another example of his creative (mis)remembering. The ship had been built only two years earlier; it was piloted by one of the most respected officers on the river; and contemporary newspapers praised it as a "magnificent," "first class," and a "very staunch and pretty packet" with "finely furnished cabins" and "superb" dining.[36]

During the twelve-day voyage from the Queen City to the Crescent City, including four days when the boat was aground on the rocks near Louisville, Sam ingratiated himself with one of the so-called knights of the tiller. Horace Bixby, only thirty at the time, "taught me how to steer the boat" during the trip, or so Sam claimed. He told Bixby that he was traveling to South America for his health, not to seek his fortune. Upon arriving in New Orleans on February 28, he quickly discovered that there was no passenger service to Brazil. In fact, he never would travel to South America. Most likely Sam did not ask Bixby to take him under his wing as a cub pilot until he had no other option. A day or two later, he found Bixby on the docks and "begged him to teach me the river." He even invoked the name of his Hannibal friend Will Bowen, who had become a pilot, as a reference. Still, Bixby was initially reluctant. Sam struck him as "a big, shaggy-haired youth with a slow, drawling speech that was provoking to anyone that happened to be in a hurry," Bixby remembered. "I told him that I did not want any assistant, as they were generally more in the way than anything else, and that the only way I would accept him would be for a money consideration." Bixby finally agreed to "instruct him till he became a competent pilot" on the lower Mississippi between St. Louis and New Orleans for $500, "not to include his expenses, except for meals on board. In port he was to look out for himself." Sam, who had no ready money except the $30 in his pocket, counteroffered Bixby his building lots in Keokuk or two thousand acres of the Tennessee land. Bixby "didn't want the real estate," as he put it, so Sam "planned a siege" before Bixby left New Orleans to pilot the *Colonel Crossman*, a 415-ton steamer, north to St. Louis. At the end of three days of onshore negotiations they compromised: $100 down, an additional $75 in six months, $75 more at the end of a year, and the balance of $250 after he earned his pilot's license and began to collect a salary. "I liked him," Bixby admitted, "and the more he talked the more anxious I got for him to try his hand." Bixby drew up a contract to formalize their agreement, which he locked away, "and neither [Sam] nor I have seen it to this day," he conceded in 1902. Sam was aboard the *Crossman* as an apprentice or cub pilot when it cast off on March 4. After it docked in St. Louis on March 15, Sam borrowed the down payment from Will Moffett and, at the age of twenty-one, launched a new career.[37]

When Sam reported to his friends and family that he planned to become a pilot on the lower Mississippi, their responses were mixed. Annie Taylor broke off their relationship, perhaps because there was no telling when he would next be in Keokuk, or perhaps because she no longer considered a boatman her social or intellectual equal, though she saved a pair of his letters to the end of her life. His niece Annie Moffett remembered that in St. Louis "everyone was running up and down stairs and sitting on the steps to talk over the news. Piloting in those days was a dramatic and well-paid profession, and in a river town it was a great honor to have a pilot in the family." His mother, on the other hand, was dismayed. "I gave him up then," she told an interviewer, "for I always thought steamboating was a wicked business and was sure he would meet bad associates."[38] According to a joke at the time, rivermen were like the river: shallowest and dirtiest at the mouth. Still, there is no evidence that Jane released Sam from his oaths to avoid gambling and drinking hard liquor—nor, for that matter, that he began to violate either oath.

CHAPTER 5

The River

When I find a well-drawn character in fiction or biography, I generally take a warm personal interest in him, for the reason that I have known him before—met him on the river.

—*Life on the Mississippi*

"I put sam to work right away," Horace Bixby boasted. "In all my time I never knew a man who took to the labor of piloting with so little effort. He was born for it, just as some men are born to make poetry and some to paint pictures." On his part, Samuel Clemens was hardly so sanguine:

> I entered upon the small enterprise of "learning" twelve or thirteen hundred miles of the great Mississippi River with the easy confidence of my time of life. If I had really known what I was about to require of my faculties, I should not have had the courage to begin. I supposed that all a pilot had to do was to keep his boat in the river, and I did not consider that that could be much of a trick, since it was so wide.

Sam was capable of prodigious feats of memory even while harboring an appalling ignorance. "Every pilot had to carry in his head thousands of details of that great river—details, moreover, that were always changing," he argued on the one hand. Or, as he explained in *Life on the Mississippi* (1883),

> I think a pilot's memory is about the most wonderful thing in the world. To know the Old and New Testaments by heart, and be able to recite them glibly, forward or backward, or begin at random anywhere in the book and recite both ways and never trip or make a mistake, is no extravagant mass of knowledge, and no marvelous facility, compared to a pilot's massed knowledge of the Mississippi and his marvellous facility in the handling of it.

On the other hand, Sam was never familiar with the technical details about the operation of a steamboat. He conceded years later that he "never learned all the parts of a boat," rather like a race car driver who could not repair his own vehicle but could keep it in a groove around the track: "Names of parts were . . . in my ear daily whose office & locality I was ignorant of, & I never inquired the meaning of those names." Neither Bixby nor Sam mentioned in retrospect that the so-called lightning pilot began to teach the river to Sam in the spring, the season of high water, when dangers to boat, cargo, passengers, and crew were negligible.[1]

In fact, piloting a steamboat at most times of the year was an extremely hazardous occupation. The boats were hardly the "floating palaces" of legend, but mostly cheaply constructed, wooden, rickety tinderboxes. As Robert Sattelmeyer explains, "Boats were profitable to the extent that they ran risks: carrying too much steam, overloading freight or passengers, running dangerous chutes to save time, venturing into rivers at marginal water levels, and so forth. . . . Not surprisingly, the life expectancy of a Mississippi steamboat was four to five years." Flimsily built with flat bottoms to glide over sandbars, steamboats might sink in as little as three or four feet of water. About a thousand steamboat accidents—on average, one every two weeks—were reported on western rivers between 1811 and 1851, and the remains of some two hundred wrecked steamboats were submerged between St. Louis and Cairo, Illinois, a distance of only about two hundred miles. As Bernard DeVoto notes, of the thousand boats that plied the Mississippi when Sam worked the river, "the soundly built boat was the exception, a product of occasional pride or responsibility; the average boat was assembled from inferior timber and machinery, thrown together with the least possible expense, and hurried out to snare her portion of the unimaginable profits before her seams opened or her boiler heads blew off. Once launched, she entered a competition ruthless and inconceivably corrupt." Captains and pilots were personally liable to criminal and civil penalties in the event of accidents, including explosions, and unless they owned part of the boat they enjoyed "minimal job security, berths that were usually transient, [and] wages that fluctuated greatly." For two years after he earned his pilot's license, Sam earned a salary equal to that of the vice president of the United States or an associate justice of the U.S. Supreme Court while at work, but his periods of employment were punctuated by unpaid layoffs and layovers. His workday was divided into six four-hour shifts—three shifts on duty, the other three devoted to sleep and a little leisure. Riverboat officers were also liable to be punished for their support of unionization, and while in port pilots were subject to the orders of their captains. Gambling and prostitution flourished on the boats and in the towns along the river, and Sam was complicit in "this trade in greed and corruption" during a formative era of his life. Yet he omitted "the squalid venery" of the boating profession, as DeVoto called it, from both his extant private letters of the period and from *Life on the Mississippi*, his most complete public account of his piloting career.[2]

Instead he romanticized his experience on the river. As early as August 1866, writing to his friend Will Bowen, whose father had been a steamboat captain, Sam averred that the pilot "obeys no man's orders & scorns all men's suggestions." Even kings were "*slaves* to other men & to circumstances" compared to the pilot. "The king *would* do this thing, & he *would* do that," he explained,

> but a cramped treasury overmasters him in the one case & a seditious people in the other. The Senator must hob-nob with canaille whom he despises, & banker, priest & statesman trim their actions by the breeze of the world's will & the world's opinion. . . . [T]he only real, independent & genuine gentlemen in the world go quietly up & down the Mississippi river, asking no homage of any one, seeking no popularity, no notoriety, & not caring a damn whether school keeps or not.

Almost a decade later, Sam echoed these sentiments in "Old Times on the Mississippi" (1875):

> I loved the profession far better than any I have followed since, and I took a measureless pride in it. The reason is plain: a pilot, in those days, was the only unfettered and entirely independent human being that lived in the earth. Kings are but the hampered servants of parliament and people; parliaments sit in chains forged by their constituency; the editor of a newspaper cannot be independent, but must work with one hand tied behind him by party and patrons, and be content to utter only half or two-thirds of his mind; no clergyman is a free man and may speak the whole truth, regardless of his parish's opinions; writers of all kinds are manacled servants of the public. We write frankly and fearlessly, but then we "modify" before we print. In truth, every man and woman and child has a master, and worries and frets in servitude; but in the day I write of, the Mississippi pilot had none.

In 1874 he admitted to Howells that, were he single, he would happily return to the river. "I am a person who would quit authorizing in a minute to go to piloting. I would rather sink a steamboat than eat, any time." In 1895 Sam described his Mississippi years as "the only period in my life . . . that I ever enjoyed," and as late as 1908 in his autobiographical dictation he declared that piloting had not been "work to me; it was play—delightful play, vigorous play, adventurous play—and I loved it." Yet two years earlier he confided to Paine that "never a month passes . . . that I do not dream of being in reduced circumstances, and obliged to go back to the river to earn a living. It is never a pleasant dream, either. I love to think about those days; but there's always something sickening about the thought that I have been obliged to go back to them."[3]

◈

Sam remained in St. Louis until April 29, 1857, when he began to apprentice under Bixby on the *Crescent City*—at 688 tons, twice the size of the *Paul Jones*, and one of the most luxurious boats on the river, outfitted (quite literally) with all the bells and whistles. As he remembered in "Old Times on the Mississippi," his "master" had been "hired to go on a big New Orleans boat, and I packed my satchel and went with him. She was a grand affair. When I stood in her pilot-house I was so far above the water that I seemed perched on a mountain; and her decks stretched so far away, fore and aft, below me, that I wondered how I could ever have considered the little 'Paul Jones' a large craft." He remembered, too, that on this cruise he thought "the highest bluff on the river between St. Louis and New Orleans—it was near Selma, Missouri—was probably the highest mountain in the world. It is four hundred and thirteen feet high." The boat docked in New Orleans on May 4, reversed course on May 8, and arrived back in St. Louis on May 15. On his second trip to the Big Easy in late May, he visited the French Market and marveled at the produce on display and the "men, women of children of every age, color and nation," a far cry from his racist observations about New York City crowds four years earlier.[4]

In all, Sam completed five round-trips between St. Louis and New Orleans by the end of August, the first three aboard the *Crescent City* with Bixby. Next he cubbed on the *Rufus J. Lackland*, at 710 tons a boat even larger than the *Crescent City*, and then the *John J. Roe*, a bulky 691-ton freighter and "delightful old tug" so sluggish, he joked, that "upstream she couldn't even beat an island" and "downstream she was never able to overtake the current." The *Roe*, piloted by Zeb Leavenworth and Beck Jolly, was so slow that "we used to forget what year it was [when] we left port" and "when she finally sunk in Madrid Bend, it was five years before the owners heard of it."[5]

Sam was enamored about this time with a pair of young women. The first was Emma Comfort Roe, the daughter of one of the owners of the *John J. Roe*. The second was the "prettiest" and "most accomplished" girl along the river, someone who lived in Napoleon, Tennessee, near Madrid Bend, Missouri (a town that has since washed away); this was likely Myra Robbins, whom he had met in St. Louis but who often visited a family farm near Napoleon and Point Pleasant, Missouri. According to Robbins's descendants, she was one of Sam's "sweethearts" and "something of a beauty." He often brought her gifts and, on one occasion, he landed his boat at Point Pleasant and "sent a beautiful decorated cake" to her. He later asked permission to court her, but her father refused because "he did not approve of river men."[6]

❖

During layovers in St. Louis, Sam resided with the Moffetts at their home on Locust Street and occasionally dined with his mother's cousin James Lampton. A lawyer by training, Cousin Jim lived "in a tinted mist of magnificent dreams," Sam remembered. According to Henry Watterson, he stood "in the relation of a second father" to Sam. He also was the model for Sam's character Colonel Sellers in *The Gilded Age* (1873) and *The American Claimant* (1892), an inveterate optimist whose get-rich-quick schemes always turned to dust. As Watterson noted, "Never such a hero [as Jim Lampton] lived in such a fool's paradise."

During his layovers in New Orleans, Sam worked as a watchman on the wharf for three dollars a night to earn his living expenses. He also acquired a smattering of the local French dialect so that he could converse with the Creoles, but not so well that he could speak it in France; in Paris a decade later Sam joked that he and his compatriots "never did succeed in making those idiots understand their own language," and in Montreal in December 1881 he similarly cracked, "I can speak French, but I cannot understand it."[7]

Sam was employed on the docks in St. Louis during the entire month of September 1857—one of the disadvantages of piloting, the periodic layoffs—before he and Bixby caught a ride on the 662-ton *William M. Morrison* on October 9, arriving in New Orleans seventeen days later. Bixby's copilot on the *Morrison* was probably Isaiah Sellers, a venerable presence on the Mississippi since 1825, during the era of keelboats. During his thirty-five-year career, Sellers piloted boats on an estimated 460 round-trips between St. Louis and New Orleans. But Sam, as usual, was unimpressed by seniority or assumptions of rank. Sellers repeatedly slept through the start of his shifts, and Sam was responsible for waking him until, on one occasion, or so goes the story, Sam was "struck square on the nose by a heavy boot, and he didn't like it much." Sam retaliated by putting live frogs in Sellers's boots and rubbing red pepper on his nose while he slept.[8] He soon exacted an even greater measure of revenge.

Sellers was a prominent antiunion man, another reason for Sam to dislike him. The St. Louis and New Orleans Pilots Association had existed since the 1840s but, according to Edgar Marquess Branch, "its push for high salaries and a stronger union began in earnest during May 1857" as Sam was apprenticing on the *Crescent City*. A resolution demanding higher salaries was signed by several pilots active in the association on August 28, the day before Sam arrived in St. Louis aboard the *Roe*. Among the signers were Bart and Will Bowen, Sam's friends from Hannibal, both of whom had become pilots; Strother Wiley, the copilot of the *Crescent City*; Beck Jolly of the *Roe*; and William Brown and George Ealer, pilots with whom Sam would serve in the months to come. In March 1859, shortly before Sam earned his pilot's license, moreover, the group was formally chartered by an act of the Missouri state legislature as the Western Boatmen's Benevolent Association (WBBA). Ten days later, the St. Louis *Missouri Democrat* reported that "nearly every pilot of any standing" on the lower Mississippi had joined the organization, which was a more aggressive federation than the typographical unions Sam had joined earlier. Unfortunately, the pilots were fighting a failing rearguard action. As a result of the Panic of 1857 and the ensuing recession, Branch notes, "river commerce on the lower Mississippi rapidly declined by the fall of 1857" and by early 1859 "even the upper Mississippi pilots, formerly employed at $1500 a month, were working for as little as $200." Still, Bixby became not only a member of the WBBA but its president. In other words, Sam's abbreviated piloting career coincided with the heyday of the WBBA. He wrote Will Bowen in 1866 that "no king ever wielded so absolute a sway over subject & domain as did that old Association. . . . It was a beautiful system—beautiful." As he later added, "it was perhaps the compactest, the completest, and the strongest commercial organization ever formed among men." The union was given its death knell when the treasurer absconded with all its money.[9]

With wages falling in the wake of the Panic, Bixby—who held licenses to pilot on the lower Mississippi, the Ohio, and the Missouri Rivers—decided to steer shallow-draft steamboats on the Missouri above St. Louis where he "could make a lot more money." Because Sam "had not wanted to learn the Missouri," Bixby added, "I struck a new bargain with him and turned the teaching job over" to pilots Brown and Ealer on the *Pennsylvania*, a three-year-old, 486-ton side-wheeler captained by John S. Kleinfelter. Sam soon despised Brown, "with his snarling ways & meannesses," but became fast friends with Ealer, who "was a prime chess player and an idolater of Shakespeare." Ealer "would play chess with anybody, even with me," Sam remembered. "Also—quite uninvited—he would read Shakespeare to me; not just casually, but by the hour, when it was his watch, and I was steering." Ealer "knew his Shakespeare as well as Euclid ever knew his multiplication table."[10] The pilothouse on the *Pennsylvania* became a classroom.

In his free time, too, Sam was an avid reader. In his autobiography he recalled reading by the light of Donati's Comet, "the most illustrious wanderer of the skies that has ever appeared in the heavens within the memory of men now living," during the autumn of 1858. "It was a wonderful spray of white light," he noted, "a light so powerful that I think it was able to cast shadows—however, necessarily it *could*, there is no occasion to seek for evidence of that; there is sufficient evidence of it in the fact that one could read . . . by that light." Abraham Lincoln similarly viewed the comet from a hotel in Jonesboro, Illinois, on the night of September 14, 1858, and Nathaniel Hawthorne observed it from the hills of Tuscany during the first week of October. While it is impossible to know what Sam read by the light of the comet, his literary tastes were catholic, even if his religion was not. He became familiar with the writings of Miguel de Cervantes, Oliver Goldsmith, Thomas Gray, Thomas Hood, Henry Wadsworth Longfellow, Thomas Babington Macaulay, Alexander Pope, Tobias Smollett, Laurence Sterne, Jonathan Swift, Voltaire, Horace Walpole, and William Wordsworth. He developed a liking for the novels of Charles Dickens, and he sprinkled allusions to *Martin Chuzzlewit*, *David Copperfield*, *Dombey and Son*, and the *Pickwick Papers* throughout his writings. He thrilled to Elisha Kane's *Arctic Explorations* (1856), and he was convinced by Delia Bacon's *The Philosophy of the Plays of Shakespeare Unfolded* (1857, with an introduction by Nathaniel Hawthorne) that Francis Bacon was the author of the plays attributed to the bard. As early as 1858 Sam wrote Orion that he considered "the grandest thing" in John Milton's *Paradise Lost* "the Arch-Fiend's terrible energy!" He read John Cleland's erotic novel *Fanny Hill* (1748) no later than 1862, and he was infatuated with the essays of Ralph Waldo Emerson that promulgated "the great law of compensation—the great law that regulates Nature's heedless agents." Or, as he explained it by analogy, "the same gust of wind that blows a lady's dress aside and exposes her ankle fills your eyes so full of sand that you can't see it."[11]

But of all authors Thomas Paine may have exerted the most influence on him. He had read Paine's "The American Crisis" as early as October 1853. As a cub pilot, he read *The Age of Reason* "with fear and hesitation, but marveling at its fearlessness and wonderful power." Years later he added that it "took a brave man before the Civil War to confess that he had read" the book. Sam spouted Paine's deist doctrines, particularly his mechanistic view of creation, until the end of his life. In his Christmas 1865 column for the San Francisco *Dramatic Chronicle*, Sam paid tribute to Paine's principled opposition to "the Christian superstition." Yet as "clear and vigorous as was his intellect," he conceded, Paine underestimated the staying power of Christianity and its resistance to rationalism. "He was nevertheless an able writer," Sam concluded, "and thoroughly honest in his convictions. Disgusted by hypocrisy and bigotry, he made war upon religion, fully believing that he was doing a good work." In *The Crusade of the Excelsior* (1887) by Bret Harte, one of Sam's friends in San Francisco in the mid-1860s, the character Martinez, modeled on Mark Twain (the names share six letters in sequence), rails against the Catholic Church and quotes Paine. In all, Sherwood Cummings argues, it is "nearly impossible to exaggerate the impact of *The Age of Reason* on the mind of Samuel Clemens." According to Minnie Brashear, Paine offered Sam "his first glimpse of what seemed to him a worthy ideal of life and thinking different to that approved in his Hannibal world." His admiration for Paine supplied him with a point of contrast between the conjoined twins Luigi and Angelo in the first chapter of *Those Extraordinary Twins* (1894): the religious skeptic Luigi reads *The Age of Reason*, while Angelo reads a seventeenth-century Christian devotional tract titled *The Whole Duty of Man*. As late as 1894 Sam criticized those "who call it a sin to respect Tom Paine or know of his great service to his race."[12]

Sam's initial service on the *Pennsylvania* (November 2–26, 1857) ended when the ship collided during a race with the *Vicksburg* some twenty-eight miles above New Orleans. Kleinfelter and the other owners of the *Pennsylvania* sued in federal court to recover $5,500 in damages and losses and, though he had not been on duty, Sam was deposed as a witness. "I am learning the river—have been learning it, now, about ten months," he testified, and affirmed that the "officers and crew which the 'Penn' had at the time of the collision were all of them capable sober and patient." Despite his testimony, the judge found "that the collision was the result of improper management on the part of the officers of the *Pennsylvania*," which meant that its owners were liable for both damages and court costs. The ship was also dry-docked for repairs until January 13, 1858.[13] Meanwhile, Sam apprenticed on two other steamboats: the *D. A. January*, on which he cubbed for Ed Montgomery (December 13–22, 1857), and the *New Falls City*, a spanking-new 880-ton side-wheeler captained by Montgomery and piloted by Leavenworth (January 14–20, 1858).

In early February 1858 Sam transferred back to the refitted *Pennsylvania* in New Orleans. After the boat finally reached St. Louis on February 14, Sam secured a job aboard the vessel for his brother Henry, who was unemployed and living alone in a St. Louis boardinghouse, as a "mud clerk" or purser's assistant. While it was an unpaid position, it offered room, board, and a chance for promotion. In fact, Horace Bixby had begun his career on the river as a mud clerk at the age of eighteen. Henry joined the crew in mid-February and performed such duties as measuring woodpiles and counting coal boxes. His first round-trip between St. Louis and New Orleans took three weeks (February 17–March 9) rather than the normal two because of freezing weather. On the day of departure, only fifteen miles below St. Louis, the crew was required "to hunt the channel" in the ice for several hours. "The next day was colder still," Sam wrote Orion and Mollie, and "I was out in the yawl twice" with crewmen sounding the channel. They were marooned on a sandbar for four hours in rain and sleet before the *Pennsylvania* rescued them. The next day, February 19, "was terribly cold," too. Sam was "out in the yawl from 4 o'clock in the morning till half past 9 without being near a fire. There was a thick coating of ice over men, yawl, ropes and everything else, and we looked like rock-candy statuary."[14]

In all, Sam and Henry made five round-trips together between St. Louis and New Orleans aboard the *Pennsylvania* from February to June 1858. These weeks were mostly memorable because Sam met his *femme idéale*—literally the girl of his dreams, the only sweetheart he was never able to forget—in the Crescent City the evening of May 16. He was instantly smitten. Laura Wright was the fourteen-year-old daughter of a county judge and "rich man," Sam remarked in 1906 (at least "as riches were estimated in that day and region"), who lived in Warsaw, Missouri, about two hundred miles west of St. Louis. She was a mere "slip of a girl," a "frank and simple and winsome child who had never been away from home in her life before." The *Pennsylvania* docked beside the *John J. Roe*, Sam's former boat, and he had gone aboard to greet his friends when "out of their midst, floating upon my enchanted vision," emerged "that comely child, that charming child." Nearly a half century later he still remembered "that unspoiled little maid, that fresh flower of the woods and the prairies." He imagined her "with perfect distinctness in the unfaded bloom of her youth, with her plaited tails dangling from her young head and her white summer frock puffing about in the wind." The descriptions are depressingly similar to Humbert Humbert's visions of the twelve-year-old girl in Vladimir Nabokov's *Lolita*. Sam's infatuation with Laura Wright is the earliest evidence of his disturbing tendency, especially pronounced late in his life, to fixate on innocent young maidens. "Confound me if I wouldn't *eat up* half a dozen of you small girls if I just had the merest shadow of a chance," he wrote Belle Stotts a couple of years later.[15]

The circumstantial evidence is substantial and almost incontrovertible that he was a latent pedophile obsessed with prepubescent lasses. Or, as Guy Cardwell puts it, Sam's "unusual attention" to young women began early, and "he and his protective circle transformed his pedophilia into a culture-approved, circumspect affection for children." At the age of twenty-five, soon after his arrival in Nevada, he ended a letter to his sister-in-law Mollie on a creepy note, asking her to kiss his six-year-old niece Jennie for him and to "tell her when she is fifteen years old I will kiss her myself . . . if she is good-looking." He conceded to the readers of the *Californian* in March 1865 that he enjoyed "gazing at handsome young girls," and as he commented in his journal in the summer of 1866, "Young girls innocent natural—*I* love 'em same as others love infants." He was particularly susceptible to their charms and freer from scrutiny by family and friends when he was on the road. During his tour of the Sandwich Islands in 1866 he noted, again in his journal, that he had seen a "dozen naked little girls bathing in brook in middle of town at noonday." The following year he wrote from New York that to "see a lovely girl of seventeen, with her saddle on her head, and her muzzle on behind, and her veil just covering the end of her nose, come tripping along in her hoopless, red-bottomed dress, like a churn on fire, is enough to set a man wild. I must drop this subject—I can't stand it." Six months later, during the *Quaker City* excursion, he admired the beautiful "scenery" in Egypt: "Naked girls in the streets—finely built." Two years later, he infantilized Olivia Langdon, his fiancée, by referring to her as "little Miss Livy," "little sweetheart," and "my child." In his autobiography he paid her a most unusual compliment: she "was slender and beautiful and girlish; she was both girl and woman. She remained both girl and woman to the last day of her life." Sam recounted an act of voyeurism in his travel narrative *A Tramp Abroad* (1880): during a fanciful raft trip on the Neckar River in Germany, he spies "a slender girl of twelve years or upward" as she bathes. "She had not time to run, but she did what answered just as well; she promptly drew a lithe young willow bough athwart her white body with one hand, and then contemplated us with a simple and untroubled interest. Thus she stood while we glided by. She was a pretty creature, and she and her willow bough made a very pretty picture." In 1902 an interviewer reported that Sam liked "pretty girls almost as well as cigars." In his late essay "Why Not Abolish It?" (1903) Sam argued for repealing the age of consent on the grounds that the seduction of women at any time in their lives was an abomination, but the argument could just as easily be construed to justify the removal of legal barriers to consorting with children. Five years later, he admitted to a most peculiar hobby: "I collect pets: young girls—girls from ten to sixteen years old; girls who are pretty and sweet and naïve and innocent—dear young creatures to whom life is a perfect joy and to whom it has brought no wounds, no bitterness, and few tears. My collection consists of gems of the first water." He referred to these girls as his "angelfish" and the club as his "aquarium." As Hamlin Hill observes, when Sam began to vacation regularly in Bermuda in 1908 his fascination with young girls "rapidly increased. . . . He would seek out for companions pre-pubescent girls, preferably those just on the verge of physical maturity, and his relentless pursuit would often drive them from him within a few days." Or as Isabel Lyon, his secretary, noted in her diary at the time, "his first interest when he goes to a new place is to find little girls. . . . [O]ff he goes with a flash when he sees a new pair of slim little legs." In June 1909, only a few months before his death, he told a pair of interviewers in Baltimore, where he delivered a graduation address at an exclusive girls' school attended by one of his angelfish, that "Pretty girls . . . are always an inspiration to me" and "I always like the young ladies, and would go a long way to be in their company."[16] Then again, no solid evidence of any actual improper behavior toward young girls has ever surfaced.

Sam was "not four inches from [Laura Wright's] elbow during our waking hours for the next three days" in May 1858, or so he recalled. Though a freighter, not a passenger boat, the *Roe* often carried guests, and Laura was the niece of William Youngblood, one of the pilots and, as Sam put it, "as fine a man as I have known." The boat also featured a piano in the cabin and, according to Sam, "a spacious boiler deck—just the place for moonlight dancing and daylight frolics."[17] He and Laura separated when the *Pennsylvania* left for St. Louis on May 20,[18] and Sam asserted in his autobiography that he "never saw her afterward" and "no word has ever passed between us since." Not true. They corresponded for the next two or three years, at least until Laura's mother began to confiscate Sam's letters (so he believed). He visited her in Warsaw at least once, in 1860. But her mother broke off the relationship soon after this visit. "The young lady has been beaten by the old one," Sam wrote to Orion, "through the romantic agency of intercepted letters, and the girl still thinks I was in fault—and always will, I reckon, for I don't see how she'll ever find out the contrary."[19]

Still, he dreamed of her every year or two for the rest of his life and covertly alluded to her in his writings. He recorded a coded reference to a dream of her in his notebook for February 1, 1865, for example: "Saw L[aura] Mark <Wrigh> Write [Wright] in a dream—ce matin-ci—in carriage— said good bye & shook hands." She was probably one of the inspirations for Becky Thatcher in *The Adventures of Tom Sawyer* (1876) and the Hartford telephone operator that Hank Morgan remembers in his dreams in *A Connecticut Yankee in King Arthur's Court* (1889). Laura married in 1862; Sam remarked laconically in 1867 that one of the "old sweethearts I have been dreaming of so long has got five children now." She eventually moved to Dallas, where she enjoyed a long teaching career in the public schools and as principal of the Temple Emanu-El school. In 1880 one of her students wrote Sam, who replied that he remembered Laura as "a very little girl, with a very large spirit, a long memory, a wise head, a great appetite for books, a good mental digestion, with grave ways, & inclined to introspection—an unusual girl." In August 1898 he wrote a story, originally titled "The Lost Sweetheart" and published posthumously under the title "My Platonic Sweetheart," about his dream lover, a type of muse. "The affection which I felt for her and which she manifestly felt for me was a quite simple fact," he declared, adding that he occasionally dreamed of her. In these dreams, both